Contents

Cette publication est également offerte en français sous le titre suivant : *Stratégie de lecture au primaire – Rapport de la table ronde des experts en lecture, 2003*.

This publication is available on the Ministry of Education's website at http://www.edu.gov.on.ca.

1 Setting the Context

A child's success in school and throughout life depends in large part on the ability to read. Educators in Ontario have the profound challenge of making reading a reality for all children.

The demands of the information age require that people be competent readers and writers if they are to participate and thrive in society. There is keen awareness that the public education system must therefore focus on providing children with the best possible reading instruction. A broad consensus now exists among researchers and educators regarding the knowledge and skills that children need in order to read, the experience that influences the development of such knowledge and skills, and the basic components of reading instruction. The purpose of this report is to draw practical conclusions from the evidence and put them in the hands of Ontario educators so that teachers can make a difference where it matters most – in the classroom.

While this report has been written primarily for teachers of Kindergarten to Grade 3, its message is important for everyone in Ontario with an interest in early reading achievement, including school and board administrators, parents, early childhood educators, community partners, and faculties of education.

The Ontario Context

Addressing the teaching of reading in Ontario begins with an understanding that there are two official languages in use in the province. Seventy-seven per cent of Ontarians have English as a first language. Franco-Ontarians, who represent 5.4 per cent of the population, constitute a minority with established historical educational rights. About 18 per cent of Ontarians have a first language other than English or French. With immigrants representing almost 25 per cent of Ontario's population, there is rich cultural diversity in many of the province's classrooms. In some large urban school boards there are 75 or more different home languages and dialects spoken by the students. This diversity in student backgrounds has many implications for early reading instruction. It is not, in itself, an obstacle to reading achievement, provided that the students have a solid foundation in their first language and support for attaining fluency in the language of instruction.

All Ontario children have a right to an English-language education. Parents with rights under section 23 of the Canadian Charter of Rights and Freedoms are also guaranteed the option of a French-language education for their children. The majority of students receiving a publicly funded education (approximately 96 per cent) are enrolled in English-language schools. Approximately nine per cent of those students attend French immersion programs. The other four per cent of Ontario students are enrolled in French-language schools.

This report affirms that the basic components of effective reading instruction are the same whether the language of instruction is English or French. However, the English and French school systems face different challenges in meeting the needs of their students.

English-language Instruction

Being in the majority, English-language schools have access to a greater variety of reading resources, especially levelled texts. Because English permeates the culture, children have daily opportunities to hear, speak, and see it – at school, on the street, in libraries, stores, and theatres, through street signs, books, magazines, newspapers, television, radio, movies, and more.

Many children come to school speaking a language other than standard English. Those who lack basic skills in English should receive additional instruction in English as a second language (ESL) or English literacy development (ELD). ESL is designed for students who have little or no fluency in English, although they are fluent in another language. ELD is for students who speak a variation of English that differs from standard English, or who have had limited prior schooling, and who need help to improve their skills in reading, writing, and oral communication. At the elementary level, ESL and ELD are support programs or interventions, rather than separate curriculum subjects. ESL/ELD students need time and assistance to develop the skills that will enable them to take full advantage of their schooling and meet the expectations of the Ontario curriculum. Because this support can be crucial in helping children to succeed, not only in reading but in all subjects, teachers need to incorporate ESL/ELD approaches and strategies throughout the curriculum.

French-language Instruction

The environment is different for children learning to read in French. Depending on the community in which they live, they may have limited exposure to the French language outside of the classroom. In addition, it is a challenge to find reading resources such as levelled texts that are adapted to the Franco-Ontarian context.

The school may be the only place where the children are exposed to French in a meaningful and consistent way. It becomes critical, then, that the school be a place steeped in French language and culture, and that support programs be strong and readily available. These programs include *Actualisation Linguistique du Français* (ALF) and *Perfectionnement du Français* (PDF). ALF is designed for children who are entitled to attend French-language schools and who have little or no fluency in French. It provides the children with the linguistic and cultural skills they need for learning. The PDF curriculum is a basic literacy program and an orientation to Canadian culture for new Canadians. These children may have had schooling in another country, but their schooling was disrupted or the system was very different from the Franco-Ontarian system, and so they lack rudimentary skills in reading, writing, and mathematics. PDF provides instructional support and familiarizes the children with both the Franco-Ontarian education system and their new social and cultural environment.

About the Early Reading Panel

The Early Reading Panel was composed of members from a wide range of constituencies involved in reading. Teachers, consultants, principals, school board administrators, academics and researchers – from English, French, and Aboriginal communities – worked together to share their expertise in the field of reading. The panel reviewed and discussed a wide range of research on reading to produce a report that outlines effective instruction and defines good practices for teaching reading to all Ontario children. The panel's guiding principles, and the key themes of this report, are summed up by four beliefs.

> **Belief #1:** *Reading instruction should be based on the evidence of sound research that has been verified by classroom practice.*

Despite the widely different conclusions and practices advocated by individual research papers or particular programs, there is an important consensus in the scientific community about the teaching of reading. Good research informs educators about the components of an effective reading program. The research is clear in showing that effective reading instruction compensates for risk factors that might otherwise prevent children from becoming successful readers.

This report takes an important step in capturing the best knowledge currently available to guide teachers in early reading instruction. Reading research needs to continue in order to ensure that our public education system has the information it needs to support improvement in the future.

Belief #2: Early success in reading is critical for children.

Reading success is the foundation for achievement throughout the school years. There is a critical window of opportunity from the ages of four to seven for children to learn to read. Research on early reading difficulties is very clear: children who continue to experience reading difficulties in Grade 3 seldom catch up later. It makes sense to detect problems early in order to avoid the escalation of problems later.

Belief #3: The teacher is the key to a child's success in learning to read.

A major consensus of research is that the ability of teachers to deliver good reading instruction is the most powerful factor in determining how well children learn to read. It is essential to recognize the critical role teachers play in preventing reading difficulties and to provide teachers at all grade levels with the best and most up-to-date knowledge and skills to teach reading and promote literacy. This understanding can help to ensure that teachers are not mere consumers of packaged products or programs, but are informed and critical thinkers who are able to make wise choices that consider the needs of the children and accomplish the goals of reading instruction.

Belief #4: In order to succeed in the classroom, teachers need the cooperation and support of instructional leaders at the school and board level who value and provide ongoing professional development.

Effective early reading instruction does not happen in isolation. It involves not only primary classroom teachers but all partners in the education system. Recognizing the importance of a system-wide, supportive approach to reading instruction, this report addresses issues regarding leadership, the development of the expertise of teachers, and the role of the home and the community. All partners play a significant role in ensuring that the conditions are right for teachers to provide effective instruction and for children to learn to the best of their ability.

Building on Common Ground

When passions for the outcome run high, and opinions are diverse, working together to find solutions that will make a meaningful difference for all children can be a huge challenge. We know what it's like: we members of the Early Reading Panel came from diverse backgrounds and brought to the table the perspectives of years of experience in our own milieus. It was indeed a challenge to recognize and address our differences, especially within the constraints of our mandate and timeline. Nevertheless, we found common ground in our passion for ensuring that all children learn to read and our conviction that good teaching makes the difference. With those fixed points to guide us, we discovered that our diversity was a strength that enabled us to see problems from many angles, draw on a wider range of resources, test our assumptions, and support our conclusions.

We recognize that this report is not an end in itself, but a contribution to an ongoing process. We offer it to the people of Ontario with our thanks for the opportunity to travel together this far on the journey.

Panel Members

Dany Laveault (Co-chair)
Professor
Faculty of Education, University of Ottawa

Bonnie McEachern (Co-chair)
Superintendent
Upper Grand District School Board

Mary Anne Alton
Superintendent
Bluewater District School Board

Chantal Bergeron
Teacher
Conseil scolaire de district des écoles catholiques du Sud-Ouest

Johanne Bourdages
Professor
Faculty of Education, University of Ottawa

Cécile Champagne-Muzar
Professor
Faculty of Education, University of Ottawa

Brenda Davis
Consultant
Six Nations

Joan Fallis
Teacher
Grand Erie District School Board

Colleen French
Superintendent
Toronto Catholic District School Board

Annie Gaudreault
Curriculum Consultant
Conseil scolaire de district du Centre Sud-Ouest

Alyson McLelland
Principal
Toronto District School Board

Mary McGuire
Curriculum Consultant
York Catholic District School Board

Thérèse McNamara
Curriculum Consultant
Simcoe County District School Board

France Nicolas
Teacher
Conseil scolaire de district catholique
du Centre-Est de l'Ontario

Julia O'Sullivan
Dean of Education, Lakehead University
National Director, Centre of Excellence for
Children and Adolescents with Special Needs

Pat Prentice
Curriculum Consultant
Durham District School Board

Angela Puma
Curriculum Consultant
Toronto Catholic District School Board

Colleen Russell
Principal
Toronto District School Board

Julie St-Onge
Assistant Professor
Faculty of Education, Laurentian University

Sharon Turnbull-Schmitt
Superintendent
Toronto District School Board

Lesly Wade-Woolley
Assistant Professor
Faculty of Education, Queen's University

Dale Willows
Professor
Institute of Child Study, Ontario Institute for
Studies in Education, University of Toronto

2 *Why Early Reading Matters*

Becoming a reader is a continuous process that begins with the development of oral language skills and leads, over time, to independent reading. Oral language – the ability to speak and listen – is a vital foundation for reading success. In every culture, children learn the language of the home as they observe, listen, speak, and interact with the adults and children in their environment. This process happens naturally and predictably in almost all cases.

While developing oral language is a natural process, learning to read is not. Children must be taught to understand, interpret, and manipulate the printed symbols of written language. This is an essential task of the first few years of school.

Reading success is the foundation for achievement throughout the school years. There is a critical window of opportunity from the ages of four to seven for learning to read. Children who successfully learn to read in the early primary years of school are well prepared to read for learning and for pleasure in the years to come. On the other hand, children who struggle with reading in Grades 1 to 3 are at a serious disadvantage. Academically, they have a much harder time keeping up with their peers, and they increasingly fall behind in other subjects. They are far more likely to suffer low self-esteem and, in their teen years, are more likely to drop out without completing high school. Children with unaddressed reading difficulties have not failed the system; the system has failed them. We now know that this is not inevitable, even for children who face significant challenges. With the right instruction and support, all children in Ontario elementary schools can learn to read.

Stages of Reading Development

As children learn to read, they progress through a series of stages. These stages are named and described in different ways by different reading specialists, but they are essentially the same.

- *In the earliest, **pre-reading** stage, children mimic the reading process without actually reading. They begin to understand what reading is about and how it works. They learn that what can be spoken can be written down and read by someone else.*

- *In the **beginning reading** stage, children learn to pay attention to the details of print and to the way that printed letters and words represent the sounds and words of oral* *language. They need to understand how the sounds of the language map onto the letters. To help children through this stage, teachers need to understand what is complex about the symbol system and present it in a way that is simple.*

- *In the* **fluency** *stage, children are able to identify words with greater skill and ease, and read with better comprehension. They need many opportunities to read texts that are predictable, patterned, and interesting in order to read words quickly and without effort. With extensive reading practice, they develop a level of fluency that enables them to read with increasing enjoyment and understanding.*

Teachers are expected to provide the conditions and instruction for children to progress from one developmental stage to the next and to inspire a love of reading, using interesting books that the children want to see, hear, and hold.

Reading to Learn

The focus of instruction in the early years is on learning to read, but over time the focus shifts to *reading to learn*. This, ultimately, is why people read and why reading matters. To reach this goal, children need help in becoming deliberate and reflective readers. They need explicit instruction in comprehension and thinking skills that will enable them to obtain and remember important ideas from the text. They also need help in integrating the information in the text with their prior knowledge in order to build on their learning and deepen their understanding.

The ease and speed with which a child progresses from *learning to read* to *reading to learn* will depend on several factors, including:

- *exposure to a rich language environment in the preschool years, with plenty of storytelling, conversation, books, and encouragement to ask and answer questions*

- *the quality and quantity of reading instruction in the early school years*

- *focused early intervention for those who are at risk of reading failure*

- *ongoing support from the family and community*

Making It Happen

Although some children learn to read at an early age with little formal instruction, it is a fallacy to assume that this happens simply because they have been exposed to "good quality" books. Most children require explicit, planned instruction – as well as plenty of exposure to suitable books – to crack the complex code of written language and become as fluent in reading as in speaking.

Effective instruction activates children's visual, auditory, and kinesthetic senses, and makes reading a living and lively experience. A good classroom program includes direct and systematic instruction, modelling and coaching, frequent practice with a variety of texts, ongoing assessment, timely feedback, and opportunities to celebrate successes. Through active engagement in the reading process, children learn ways to use their growing knowledge and skills flexibly and in combination. This enables them to read with greater fluency and comprehension. Over time, children demonstrate an increasing sophistication in their ability to read more complex texts and solve problems when the meaning is unclear. They are able to reflect on and communicate their understanding and reasoning about the reading material.

Laying a Strong Foundation

The best time for children to start learning to read is when they are very young, usually at the preschool level. In the early years – whether at home, in child care, in a preschool program, or in Junior and Senior Kindergarten – children gain a definite advantage when they are given opportunities to engage in purposeful oral language and early print activities. These activities include:

- *observing others reading*

- *enjoying and discussing a variety of books that are read aloud by others*

- *experiencing and pretending to read predictable and familiar books, alphabet books, poems, rhymes, and more*

- *acting out stories, retelling familiar stories, and singing songs*

- *sharing experiences with adults and talking about those experiences*

- *observing print in the environment and connecting print with spoken words and their meaning*

- *understanding book conventions and concepts about print (e.g., that a book has a front and a back)*

- *recognizing that words are made up of sounds, and manipulating those sounds through rhyming games, sound substitution games, alliterations, and more*

- *building new vocabulary through books, experiences, and interactions*

Through these activities, children improve their oral language skills and become involved in the joy of reading.

Reading in a Second Language

Strong oral language is the base on which reading success is built. Whether or not the child's first language matches the language of instruction, a rich background in oral language will help to develop a strong foundation for reading. Children whose first language differs from the language of instruction will need additional support to build their oral language skills in the language of instruction as they learn to read. If they do not have access outside the school to rich language experiences in the language of instruction, the school is expected to fill the void. This is particularly true for French-language schools, because their students are less likely to be exposed to the French language and culture outside of school.

3 *Effective Reading Instruction*

Effective classroom instruction in the early grades is key to creating strong, competent readers and to preventing reading difficulties. When a child enters school, it is the teacher's role to provide effective reading instruction. Although many others share responsibility for creating a supportive learning environment, it is the teacher who has the greatest opportunity and most direct responsibility for providing the instruction that inspires and enables the child to become a lifelong reader.

In the past 30 years, much research has been conducted on how children learn to read and on the most effective strategies for supporting reading achievement. Recently there has been a convergence of evidence about the knowledge, skills, and supports that children need to become proficient readers and about how to deliver these in the classroom. With this evidence to inform their practices, teachers can now be better equipped than ever to plan and deliver effective reading instruction, and to involve the whole school, the home, and the community in helping every child become a successful reader by the end of Grade 3.

The foundations of good reading are the same for all children, regardless of their gender, background, or special learning needs. All children use the same processes in learning to read. Some will need more help than others and may need more instruction in one reading skill than another, but all children must ultimately master the same basic skills for fluency and comprehension.

The focus of this report is on reading instruction in primary classrooms, but reading does not happen in isolation. The three strands of the language curriculum – oral and visual communication, reading, and writing – are interwoven. Oral language is the basis for literacy development, particularly in the early primary years. Children need oral language and writing skills in order to be proficient in reading; conversely, they need to be proficient readers in order to further develop their oral language and writing skills. Although instructional strategies for oral language and writing are not discussed in detail here, they are essential for teaching children to read. They need to be integrated in all subject areas and encouraged at every opportunity.

This section of the report outlines the essential, interactive components of effective reading instruction. It addresses the following: the goals of reading instruction; knowledge and skills that children need to become effective readers; instruction; and assessment, evaluation, and reporting.

The Framework for Effective Early Reading Instruction (figure 1) reminds teachers to include all of these components in their classroom reading programs to ensure that their students become successful readers and achieve the expectations of the Ontario language curriculum. All of the components are important, but the degree of emphasis on specific knowledge and skills will depend on the child's age, grade, and stage of reading development.

Figure 1. A Framework for Effective Early Reading Instruction

The Goals of Reading Instruction

FLUENCY • COMPREHENSION • MOTIVATION

All children become fluent readers who comprehend what they are reading, can apply and communicate their knowledge and skills in new contexts, and have a strong motivation to read.

The Knowledge and Skills That Children Need for Proficiency in Reading

Oral language
Prior knowledge and experience
Concepts about print
Phonemic awareness
Letter-sound relationships

Vocabulary for reading
Semantics and syntax
Metacognition and comprehension strategies
Higher-order thinking skills

Assessment, Evaluation, Reporting, Target Setting, and Improvement Planning

Classroom level
School level
Board level
Provincial level

Instructional Approaches to the Teaching of Reading

Phonics and word study
Read-aloud
Shared reading
Guided reading
Guided comprehension
Independent reading

Teaching Practices That Support Early Reading Achievement

- Balance of direct instruction, guided instruction, independent learning, and practice.
- Large group, small group, and individual instruction, discussion, and collaboration.
- Variety of assessment and evaluation techniques to inform program planning and instruction.
- Integration of phonics and word study in reading, writing, and oral language instruction.
- Uninterrupted literacy block each day.
- Parental and community involvement.

- High-quality literature and levelled texts.
- Variety of genres, narratives, informational texts, and electronic media.
- Authentic and motivating literacy experiences and learning activities.
- Interventions for students at risk of not learning to read.
- Supportive classroom culture and environment that promotes higher-order thinking skills.
- Guidance, coaching, and feedback for students.
- Effective classroom organization and management.

Goals of Reading Instruction

Reading is the process of constructing meaning from a written text. Effective early reading instruction enables all children to become fluent readers who comprehend what they are reading, can apply and communicate their knowledge and skills in new contexts, and have a strong motivation to read.

The framework in figure 1 identifies three main goals for reading instruction:

- **Fluency** *is the ability to identify words accurately and read text quickly with good expression. Fluency comes from practice in reading easy books about familiar subjects. These texts primarily contain familiar, high-frequency words so that the child will encounter few unfamiliar words. As children develop fluency, they improve in their ability to read more expressively, with proper phrasing, thus gaining more of the text's meaning.*

- **Comprehension** *is the ability to understand, reflect on, and learn from text. To ensure that children develop comprehension skills, effective reading instruction builds on their prior knowledge and experience, language skills, and higher-level thinking.*

- **Motivation to read** *is the essential element for actively engaging children in the reading process. It is the fuel that lights the fire and keeps it burning. Children need to be immersed in a literacy-rich environment, filled with books, poems, pictures, charts, and other resources that capture their interest and make them want to read for information and pleasure.*

These three goals are interconnected, and the strategies for achieving them work together synergistically.

Knowledge and Skills for Reading

Children need to learn a variety of skills and strategies in order to become proficient readers. In the earliest stages, they need to understand what reading is about and how it works – that what can be spoken can also be written down and read by someone else. Some children will have already grasped the basic concepts before entering school, but many will need explicit instruction to set the context for reading. When children first experience formal reading instruction in school, they need to learn specific things about oral language, letters, and words. They need to understand how print works, and be able to connect print with the sounds and words in oral language. Once they can demonstrate these skills, the emphasis shifts to developing fluency. Fluency at this level involves recognizing words in text quickly and without effort. This will allow the children to read with increasing enjoyment and understanding. Fluency is critical if they are to move from *learning to read* to *reading to learn*. The role of primary teachers, working as a team, is to move children from the earliest awareness of print to the reading-to-learn stage, where they will become independent, successful, and motivated readers.

According to research, the knowledge and skills that children need in order to read with fluency and comprehension include: oral language; prior knowledge and experience; concepts about print; phonemic awareness; letter-sound relationships; vocabulary; semantics and syntax; metacognition; and higher-order thinking skills. These are not isolated concepts taught in a lock-step sequence; they are interrelated components that support and build on each other.

Oral Language

Children come to reading with considerable oral language experience. They acquire most of what they know about oral language by listening and speaking with others, including their families, peers, and teachers. Through experience with oral language, children build the vocabulary, semantic knowledge (awareness of meaning), and syntactic knowledge (awareness of structure) that form a foundation for reading and writing. Children who are proficient in oral language have a solid beginning for reading. This knowledge allows them to identify words accurately and to predict and interpret what the written language says and means.

Not all children begin school with a solid foundation in oral language. Some children come from language-impoverished backgrounds where they have little opportunity to develop a rich vocabulary and complex language structures. These children may or may not be native speakers of English or French. Other children have a history of speech and language difficulties and may have smaller vocabularies and less mature grammar than their peers. Children with mild hearing impairment may find it difficult to make fine distinctions between similar speech sounds. These children require instruction that increases their oral language abilities (including phonemic awareness, vocabulary, listening comprehension, and the oral expression of ideas) in conjunction with reading skills.

It is important to remember that, although some children who speak a first language or dialect that is different from the language of instruction may begin school with a limited vocabulary in the language of instruction, they may have strong conceptual knowledge and a rich language foundation on which to build fluency and comprehension in their new language. The key for these children is to provide support for building strong bridges from the known to the new.

For the benefit of all children, teachers should constantly model language structures that are more elaborate and varied than the ones children use outside of school, and should engage the children in using these structures and variations for themselves. Children need frequent opportunities to ask and answer questions, participate in discussions, and classify information in order to develop their capacity for higher-order, critical thinking.

The importance of oral language as a foundation for reading has significant implications in the French-language school system. Because French is used by a minority of Ontarians, children have limited opportunities to hear and speak it outside of school. For some children, school is the only place where French is used systematically. It is therefore imperative that the school provide an environment where children can experience the language in a living way. Children must have many opportunities to speak French, both in the classroom and during extracurricular activities. By allowing time for in-class discussions and by providing a rich vocabulary, teachers help children to develop their fluency in French.

Prior Knowledge and Experience

In order that children may understand what they are reading, it is important that they come to the text with a variety of experiences that will allow them to appreciate the concepts embedded in the text. These experiences enable them to anticipate the content, and such anticipation leads to easier decoding of the text and deeper understanding of its meaning.

Prior knowledge and experience refers to the world of understanding that children bring to school. Research on the early stages of learning indicates that children begin to make sense of their world at a very young age. In many parts of Ontario, children enter school from a variety of countries and cultures. Thus their prior knowledge and experiences may differ considerably from those of their classmates and teachers, and they may find it difficult to relate to the context and content of the resources generally used in Ontario classrooms. On the other hand, they may have a wealth of knowledge and experiences that can enhance the learning of their classmates. Teachers need to be aware of children's backgrounds, cultures, and experiences in order to provide appropriate instruction. By creating rich opportunities for all children to share prior knowledge and related experiences, teachers will engage the interest of children from various backgrounds and ensure that they will better understand what they read.

Concepts About Print

When children first encounter print, they are not aware that the symbols on the page represent spoken language or that they convey meaning. The term *concepts about print* refers to awareness of how language is conveyed in print. These concepts include: directionality (knowing that English or French text is read from left to right and top to bottom); differences between letters and words (words are made of letters, and there are spaces between words); awareness of capitalization and punctuation; diacritic signs (e.g., accents in French); and common characteristics of books (such as the front/back, title, and author).

Young children can be taught these concepts by interacting with and observing experienced readers (including teachers and family members) who draw their attention to print and give them opportunities to demonstrate their understanding of the concepts. Teachers need to provide children with a variety of printed materials for practice, including books, big books, charts, and environmental print (such as signs and labels).

Phonemic Awareness

Children need to learn that the *words we say* are made up of sounds. This understanding is called phonemic awareness. Research has confirmed that phonemic awareness is a crucial foundation for word identification. Phonemic awareness helps children learn to read; without it, children struggle and continue to have reading difficulties. The evidence also shows that phonemic awareness can be taught and that the teacher's role in the development of phonemic awareness is essential for most children.

> *Phonemic awareness and letter-sound knowledge account for more of the variation in early reading and spelling success than general intelligence, overall maturity level, or listening comprehension (National Reading Panel, 2000). They are the basis for learning an alphabetic writing system. (Learning First Alliance, 2000, p. 14)*

Children who have phonemic awareness are able to identify and manipulate the individual sounds in oral language. They demonstrate this, for example, in recognizing that the spoken word "ship" consists of three distinct sounds: sh + i + p. In English there are about 44 speech sounds and in French 36. The number of individual speech sounds in other languages varies. In learning a second language, children may encounter speech sounds that do not exist in their home language, and so they may need more time to develop phonemic awareness in the language of instruction.

In order for children to develop phonemic awareness, teachers need to engage them in playing with and manipulating the sounds of language. This can be accomplished through songs, rhymes, and activities that require children to blend individual sounds together to form words in their heads, and by breaking words they hear into their constituent sounds. Blending and segmentation of speech sounds in oral language provide an essential foundation for reading and writing. Phonemic awareness prepares children for decoding and encoding the sounds of the language in print.

Letter-Sound Relationships

Building on the foundation of phonemic awareness and concepts about print, children are ready to understand that there is a way to connect the sounds they hear with the print on the page in order to make meaning. In both the English and French writing systems, one letter may not necessarily represent one single sound, and so it is important that children receive systematic and explicit instruction about correspondences between the speech sounds and individual letters and groups of letters.

Phonics instruction teaches children the relationships between the letters (graphemes) of written language and the individual sounds (phonemes) of spoken language. Research has shown that systematic and explicit phonics instruction is the most effective way to develop childrens' ability to identify words in print.

Vocabulary for Reading

Children need a broad vocabulary of words that they understand and can use correctly to label their knowledge and experiences. The breadth and depth of a child's vocabulary provide the foundation for successful comprehension. Oral vocabulary refers to words that are used in speaking or recognized in listening. Reading vocabulary refers to words that are recognized or used in print.

Vocabulary development involves coming to understand unfamiliar words and being able to use them appropriately. It is a huge challenge for children to read words that are not already part of their oral vocabulary. To develop their students' vocabulary, teachers need to model how to use a variety of strategies in order to understand what words mean (e.g., using the surrounding context, or using smaller, meaningful parts of words, such as prefixes or suffixes). Good teaching includes selecting material for reading aloud that will expand children's oral vocabulary, and providing opportunities for children to see and use new reading vocabulary in different contexts. Recent research on vocabulary instruction indicates that children learn most of their vocabulary indirectly by engaging daily in oral language, listening to adults read to them, and reading extensively on their own. Research also shows that some vocabulary must be taught directly. This can be done by introducing specific words before reading, providing opportunities for active engagement with new words, and repeating exposure to the vocabulary in many contexts.

Even children who have a very extensive oral vocabulary may have great difficulty reading words in print because they have a small reading vocabulary. The reading vocabulary – often referred to as *sight* vocabulary – is determined mainly by how many times a child has seen those words in print. Children who read a lot have a large pool of words they recognize immediately on sight; children who do little reading have a limited sight vocabulary. To increase their students' sight vocabularies so they can recognize a large proportion of the words in print, teachers need to focus their instruction and practice on the most commonly used words in the language.

Semantics, Syntax, and Pragmatics

Although words alone carry meaning, reading for the most part involves the deciphering of phrases and sentences, which depends on both the words and how those words are organized. Therefore, it is important to spend instructional time not only on the meanings of individual words but also on the meanings of phrases and complete sentences.[1]

Semantics refers to meaning in language, including the meaning of words, phrases, and sentences. *Syntax* refers to the predictable structure of a language and the ways that words are combined to form phrases, clauses, and sentences. Syntax includes classes of words (such as noun, verb, and adjective) and their functions (such as subject and object). Semantic and syntactic knowledge are important because they help children to identify words in context and lead to deeper levels of comprehension. Beginning readers may not need to be able to define *noun* or *verb*, but they need to understand that a word (like "snow") can represent a thing or an action, depending on the context. Providing this explicit understanding can be especially important for children whose first language is not the language of instruction.

Teachers need to model correct sentence structures so that children can learn to anticipate these structures when reading print. Opportunities should be provided for children to become familiar with and use the specific terminology for basic parts of speech (e.g., noun,

1. In French, the written language differs from the oral language, and this difference can have an impact on reading. Certain alphabetic symbols may be present in writing but not be pronounced (e.g., in *ils marchent*).

verb, adjective, adverb) to facilitate instruction. Teachers also need to familiarize children with a variety of language structures and encourage their use of longer, more complex sentences.

Pragmatics, which is introduced in the later primary years, is the study of how people choose what they say or write from the range of possibilities available in the language, and how listeners or readers are affected by those choices. Pragmatics involves understanding how the context influences the way sentences convey information. A sentence can have different purposes depending on the situation or context in which it is used. It can be a mere statement or affirmation, but it can also be a warning, a promise, a threat, or something else. Readers with pragmatic knowledge and skills are able to decipher these different intents from the context.

Teachers in the later primary years need to show children how to use context clues that surround an unfamiliar word to help figure out the word's meaning. Because children learn most word meanings indirectly, or from context, it is important that they learn to use context clues effectively. However, context clues alone are not enough; the teacher will need to teach other word-meaning strategies to develop the child's ability to learn new words.

Metacognition and Comprehension Strategies

Comprehension is the reason for reading. If readers can identify the words but do not understand what they are reading, they have not achieved the goal of reading comprehension. To gain a good understanding of the text, children must bring to it the foundational knowledge and skills of oral language, prior knowledge and experience, concepts about print, phonemic awareness, letter-sound relationships, vocabulary, semantics, and syntax. They must integrate what they bring to the text with the text itself. In order to *read to learn*, children need to use problem-solving, thinking processes. They must reflect on what they know and need to know (metacognition) and draw on a variety of comprehension strategies to make sense of what they read.

Good readers plan and monitor their reading at a metacognitive level. What they are doing is thinking about the strategies they need to make sense of the text. When they run into difficulty, they evaluate their reading to determine the best strategy for improving their understanding of the text. Children who read at a metacognitive level know the strategies that affect their own reading (e.g., decoding hard words, connecting text with prior experiences, understanding word meanings, identifying main ideas, drawing inferences from the text, and synthesizing information). These children use a variety of strategies to decode and understand text and to know when and why to apply particular strategies (e.g., knowing they do not need to use a phonics strategy to identify a word they already know by sight). Their understanding of the text extends beyond the literal.

Teachers play an important role in modelling how to think metacognitively to help children figure out what they know and what they need to know. Comprehension strategies are conscious plans that readers use to make sense of the text. Research has pointed to some effective comprehension strategies that teachers can use to help children gain meaning from the text. These include teaching children to ask questions such as those found in table 1.

Table 1. Asking Questions to Promote Comprehension

Question	Purpose of the question
How does this connect with what I already know?	activating relevant, prior knowledge before, during, and after reading
What pictures does this text create in my mind?	creating visual and other sensory images from text during and after reading
How can I use the pictures and the text to help me understand?	drawing inferences from the text to form conclusions, make critical judgements, and create unique interpretations
What are the most important ideas and themes in the text?	using the main ideas to provide clues about meaning
How can I say this in my own words?	synthesizing what they read
Does this make sense?	monitoring comprehension
Why did the author write this?	exploring the author's intent
How is this text like other texts that I have read?	finding clues in the text's structure

Higher-Order Thinking Skills

The development of higher-order thinking skills is essential throughout the primary grades. In the early stages of reading development, higher-order thinking can be developed at the oral level through teacher read-alouds and shared reading. In the *reading-to-learn* stage, classroom teachers need to ask children questions that challenge them to move beyond what they recall of the text and on to what they understand through application, analysis, synthesis, and evaluation. Children need to have opportunities to manipulate and criticize the concepts and understandings of what they have read. Children will formulate opinions and substantiate their thinking. They are no longer simply passive readers.

Bloom's taxonomy is a useful tool for helping teachers engage children in higher-order thinking when they read.[2] Table 2 shows that, as children apply higher-order thinking, they are able to draw more meaning from what they learn and apply the learning in more sophisticated ways. Although thinking skills alone do not make a child an effective reader, they are essential for reading. Higher-order thinking is what enables children to achieve the provincial standard for reading, which is level 3 in the Ontario curriculum.

Table 2. Using Bloom's Taxonomy in Reading Instruction

Level	Definition	What the Student Will Do:
Evaluation	Judging the value of ideas, materials, or products	Give value. Make choices. Arrange ideas. Judge ideas. Present choices.
Synthesis	Putting together constituent parts or elements to form a new whole	Use prior knowledge to activate new knowledge. Change existing ideas. Create new ideas.
Analysis	Breaking down an idea into its constituent parts	Look at parts. See relationships. Organize parts.
Application	Using information in new situations or to solve a new problem. Uses knowledge.	Apply previously learned information to another situation.
Comprehension	Understanding the information being communicated but not relating it to other material or ideas	Organize previously learned material in order to rephrase it, describe it in own words, explain it, or predict implications or effects on the basis of the known facts.
Knowledge (memory)	Learning the information	Recall or recognize bits of information.

---

2. Bloom's taxonomy is a widely used way of classifying educational objectives, developed in the 1950s by a group of researchers headed by Benjamin Bloom of the University of Chicago.

Instruction

Read-aloud, shared reading, guided reading, guided comprehension, independent reading, phonics, and word study provide instruction that gives children the opportunity to experience and enjoy authentic texts and to practise the skills and strategies necessary for fluency and comprehension.

No single skill in this complex interaction is sufficient on its own, and the teacher must be careful not to overemphasize one skill at the expense of others.

Reading is a meaning-making process that involves a great deal of thinking, problem solving, and decision making by both the teacher and the child. Comprehensive reading instruction teaches the child to use a variety of skills to decode, read fluently, and understand the text. No single skill in this complex interaction is sufficient on its own, and the teacher must be careful not to overemphasize one skill at the expense of others. It is important that teachers understand the interdependent nature of the skills being taught, and that competent readers integrate all sources of information as they engage in reading meaningful texts.

The teacher should provide children with planned activities for before, during, and after reading. For example:

- *Before beginning to read, the teacher and students establish the purpose for reading. Together they consider what they already know about the topic or genre and use the title, headings, table of contents or index, and new, unfamiliar vocabulary to enhance their predictions.*

- *During reading, the students respond to the text by searching for meaning, identifying the main ideas, predicting and verifying predictions, and building a coherent interpretation of the text. Students bring their experiences of the world and literature into the reading activity. The teacher directs the attention of students to subtleties in the text, points out challenging words and ideas, and identifies problems and encourages the students to predict solutions.*

- *After reading, the students reflect on their learning as they apply the knowledge acquired during reading, or transfer that knowledge to other contexts (e.g., by retelling, summarizing, creating graphic organizers, or putting pictures in sequential order).*

With all of this instruction, the teacher provides continuous role modelling, coaching, guiding, and feedback, and is always building on the children's prior knowledge and experiences. The teacher also ensures that children are focused and engaged in the reading process, and monitors their time on task.

Phonics and Word Study

Research has shown that phonics and word study are valuable strategies for improving children's ability to recognize words and decode text. Although these skills alone are not enough, they are essential building blocks for becoming an effective reader. **They may be taught out of context but must be practised in authentic contexts, and reading material that is engaging and meaningful for the children should be used.**

Phonics is a systematic instructional approach that links the foundation of phonemic awareness with children's growing knowledge of letter-sound relationships to enable children to decode words and read. Instruction begins with the most common and more easily discerned letter-sound relationships and progresses to more complex spelling patterns, which include larger chunks of words, such as syllables. Teachers need to introduce the letter-sound correspondences in a planned, sequential manner so that children have time to learn, practise, and master them. Letter formation is a part of phonics instruction that reinforces children's memory for letter-sound correspondences. To understand the usefulness of letter-sound correspondences and letter formation, children need to apply their knowledge by seeing, saying, and printing words in interesting and authentic contexts.

Word study gives children the opportunity to practise high-frequency words so that they can read them automatically (word identification), and to learn word-solving strategies so that they will be able to read partially familiar or unfamiliar words (word knowledge). Word study improves the child's ability to decode words independently, which is important for both fluency and comprehension. The teacher provides the children with an organized environment that includes charts, lists, word walls, and other resources. Activities can involve the whole class, small groups, or children working independently, and may include: searching for big words or mystery words; recognizing whole words, word parts, root words, and compound words; adding prefixes and suffixes; using known words to get to unknown words; and recognizing letter patterns.

To become fluent readers, children need to be able to read high-frequency words automatically. The most common words in texts include articles, pronouns, prepositions, conjunctions, and everyday verbs such as *to be* and *to have*. The strategies for teaching these words are different from the strategies for teaching more engaging but less frequent words, such as the names of people and the words for colours and interesting concepts. A word like *dinosaur*, for example, represents an interesting idea, and so children are more likely to remember it and recognize it when they see it in print.

Lists of grade-appropriate sight words should be used to guide instruction. Sight words need to be selected for their frequency of occurrence in print. **Teachers need to expose children regularly to these most common words and give children plenty of meaningful practice in reading them in well-written books on engaging topics, so that children are able to recognize the words instantly by sight.** If teachers provide enough opportunities for practice, children will develop the ability to read many sight words that are phonetically irregular, and will have mastered a large proportion of the words they will encounter in books.

Read-aloud

In read-aloud(s) the teacher reads to the whole class or to a small group, using material that is at the listening comprehension level of the children. The content may focus on a topic related to a curriculum expectation in another subject area, such as mathematics, science, or social studies.

Reading aloud to children helps them to develop a love of good literature, motivation to pursue reading on their own, and familiarity with a variety of genres, including non-fiction. It provides them with new vocabulary, exposes them to a variety of literature, and contributes to their oral and written language development. Reading aloud should occur every day in the early stage of reading instruction to stimulate the children's interest in books and reading.

Shared Reading

In shared reading the teacher guides the whole class or a small group in reading enlarged text that all the children can see – for example, a big book, an overhead, a chart, a poster, or a book. The text can be read several times, first *for* the children and then *with* the children joining in. Shared reading involves active participation and considerable interaction on the part of students and teachers. It is both enjoyable and motivating for children. The teacher takes into account the difficulty of the text and the skills, knowledge, and experiences of the children in structuring this activity.

Shared reading provides the teacher with the opportunity to model effective reading; promote listening comprehension; teach vocabulary; reinforce concepts about books and print and letter-sound relationships; and build background knowledge on a range of subjects.

Shared reading provides a bridge to guided reading. It should occur daily in the early stages of reading instruction and less frequently in later stages.

Guided Reading

Guided reading is a small-group, teacher-directed activity. It involves using carefully selected books at the children's instructional level. The teacher supports a small group of children as they talk, read, and think their way through a text. Children can be grouped for guided reading by reading ability or specific instructional goals. The group composition is fluid and changes according to the teacher's observations and assessments.

Guided reading provides opportunities to integrate children's growing knowledge of the conventions of print, of letter-sound relationships, and of other foundational skills in context. Through modelling and instruction, guided reading enables teachers to extend children's vocabulary development and their knowledge and use of appropriate comprehension strategies. It gives the teacher the opportunity to observe reading behaviours, identify areas of need, and allow children to develop more independence and confidence as they practise and consolidate reading behaviours and skills.

Guided reading provides a bridge to independent reading and can help children develop the necessary higher-order thinking skills.

Comprehension

Children learn comprehension skills in a variety of situations, using many levels of texts and different text types. The focus of guided comprehension is on direction, instruction, application, and reflection.

Focused instruction in comprehension skills – such as previewing; self-questioning; making links to self, text, and others; visualizing; using graphophonic, syntactic, and semantic cueing systems; monitoring, summarizing, and evaluating – is provided first. The children then apply the comprehension strategies in teacher-guided small groups and student-facilitated comprehension activities, such as literature circles, questioning the author, or reciprocal teaching.

Children work with varying degrees of support and use texts at their instructional level and independent level of reading. The teacher and the children reflect on performance, share experiences, and set new goals for learning. The levelled texts and the organization of the small group will change as the children's knowledge and reading skills increase.

Independent Reading

During purposeful and planned independent reading, the children choose their own books according to their interest and ability. The text should be chosen carefully so that each child can read with a high degree of success. Children can be taught to select appropriate independent reading material and can share this task with the teacher. Emergent readers can use this independent reading time to practise reading small, predictable stories, as well as books that have been used in shared and guided reading.

When teachers plan independent reading for children, they need to provide children with time to engage in discussion and reflection. Independent reading is preceded and followed by discussion and dialogue with the teacher and/or peers. The teacher is always observing, listening, and gathering information about the children's reading behaviour.

Purposeful and planned independent reading provides opportunities for children to build self-confidence, reinforce skill development, enhance fluency, build memory for language structures and vocabulary, and promote comprehension and the motivation to read. In addition, independent reading gives children time to get more information about a specific subject of interest.

It is important to note that the American National Reading Panel, in *Put Reading First*, their comprehensive meta-analysis of reading research, found considerable evidence to support having children read aloud with guidance and feedback, but no evidence to confirm that instructional time spent on silent independent reading with minimal guidance and feedback improves reading fluency and overall reading achievement (Center for the Improvement of Early Reading Achievement [CIERA], 2001, p. 25). This does not mean that teachers should abandon independent reading in the classroom, but they should use texts that match the child's independent reading level and ensure that each child receives feedback (from the teacher, a peer, or a volunteer) to enhance fluency, comprehension, and the motivation to read. These practices help children to decode with increasing fluency and comprehension.

Assessment, Evaluation, and Reporting

There is a direct and continuous link between teaching and assessment. Ongoing assessment must be frequent, well-planned, and organized, so that teachers are able to help each child move towards his or her full potential in reading. Assessment often involves techniques that teachers already use, such as observations and checklists. Knowing the developmental stages of reading, the associated reading skills, and the components and strategies of effective reading instruction helps the teacher to administer the right assessment and evaluation tools and interpret the results correctly. This knowledge, together with the assessment data, enables teachers to provide differentiated instruction in order to ensure the best learning opportunities for all children, through direct, explicit instruction – either in large groups, in small groups, or at the individual level, depending on the children's needs. Timely assessment is also important for identifying the small percentage of children who cannot be adequately served by good classroom instruction and who will need interventions and extra support to help them acquire the knowledge and skills for reading.

> *Assessment begins with what children know; the evidence for what they know is in what they can do. (Fountas and Pinnell, 1996, p. 73)*

Assessment

Assessment includes gathering, recording, and analysing information about a child's knowledge and skills and, where appropriate, providing descriptive feedback to help the child improve. (Assessment is different from evaluation, which involves making an informed judgement about a child's achievement at a point in time.)

- Diagnostic assessment *occurs before reading instruction begins so that the child's prior learning and current reading level can be identified and instructional priorities for the child can be determined. Diagnostic assessment can inform the teacher about detailed strategies that the child uses in the reading process. On the basis of this structured observation of the child's progress, the teacher plans the next steps in learning. Diagnostic reading tools include running records, observation surveys, cloze texts, miscue analysis, and retells.*

- Formative assessment *occurs on an ongoing basis to track the child's progress towards achievement targets. It is formative in the sense that it provides information about learning that is still forming or in progress. The child may receive the feedback immediately or at a specific stage in the learning process. Formative assessment helps*

Instead of teaching in a whole-class fashion to a hypothetical average student, we need to take into account the range of development within our classrooms, designing a curriculum that meets all our children where they are and takes each child further. Our classroom-based system of assessment should wreak havoc with any instructional plan that doesn't allow us the elasticity and breadth necessary to teach the full range of readers. Our assessments should nudge us, as teachers, to look at all our children and their work, and to look at ourselves and our work.
(Calkins, 2001, p. 157)

the teacher to make programming decisions, such as whether and how to adapt instruction to meet the needs of specific children. The majority of assessment time is spent on formative assessment. Resources include teacher observations, student portfolios, student logs, and self-reflection activities.

- *Summative assessment occurs at the end of a learning module or specific time period. Its purpose is to provide information needed to make judgements (evaluations) about student understandings. The tools for summative assessment include tests and performance-based tasks.*

Choosing Assessment Strategies

Young children show their understanding by doing, showing, and telling. Assessment strategies need to capture this doing, showing, and telling by watching, listening, and probing. Hence, observation is an integral part of all other assessment strategies. Reading assessments should not generally require the child to use writing strategies.

Table 3 gives examples of assessment strategies that can help a teacher to assess specific reading skills. Some of these strategies, such as running records, miscue analysis, and cloze procedure, are described in the Ontario Ministry of Education's *Ontario Curriculum – Exemplars, Grades 1–8: Reading* (2000, pp. 319–328).

Table 3. Instruction and Related Assessment Strategies for Reading

Phonics and Word Study	Read-Aloud
What Can Be Assessed? • Letter-sound knowledge • Ability to hear sounds within words • Ability to use spelling approximations • Ability to use conventional spelling • Strategies for pronouncing and spelling unfamiliar words • Vocabulary development	**What Can Be Assessed?** • Motivation to read • Word knowledge • Comprehension strategies
Assessment Tools and Strategies • Letter-sound knowledge • Alphabet knowledge • Word lists • Independent writing samples	**Assessment Tools and Strategies** • Teacher observation • Question/answer related to word knowledge, sentence knowledge, comprehension • Comprehension at a story level

Shared Reading	Guided Reading
What Can Be Assessed? • Motivation to read • Comprehension strategies • Word knowledge	**What Can Be Assessed?** • Sight word knowledge • Accuracy in analysing and decoding unfamiliar words (in and out of context) • Reading fluency/rate • Accuracy in reading connected text • Comprehension strategies
Assessment Tools and Strategies • Teacher observation • Question/answer related to word knowledge, sentence knowledge, comprehension • Retell	**Assessment Tools and Strategies** • Running records • Word lists • Retelling • Teacher observation • Developmental continua • Conference

Guided Comprehension	Independent Reading
What Can Be Assessed? • Motivation to read • Comprehension	**What Can Be Assessed?** • Motivation to read • Comprehension strategies • Reading fluency/rate • Ability to read high-frequency words on sight • Strategies for activating prior knowledge • Strategies for developing vocabulary
Assessment Tools and Strategies • Attitude surveys • Interest inventories • Literacy histories • Motivation profiles • Reader/writer self-perception scales • Miscue analysis • Observation	**Assessment Tools and Strategies** • Running records • Word lists • Retelling • Teacher observation • Student portfolio • Reading log/journal • Developmental continua • Conference/interview • Literature circles

Linking With the Curriculum Expectations

The Kindergarten curriculum identifies ten expectations for reading, but does not distinguish categories or levels of achievement. (See *The Kindergarten Program* [Ontario Ministry of Education, 1998, pp. 14–15].) For Grades 1 to 3, the expectations become more specific. Teachers assess children not only for individual reading skills, such as phonemic awareness, concepts about print, and vocabulary, but also according to the four categories of achievement from the Ontario language curriculum, which are reasoning, communication, organization of ideas, and application of language conventions.

Evaluation

Evaluation is an informed judgement about the quality of a child's work at a point in time. For children in Kindergarten, the evaluation is largely a description of what the teacher has observed in the classroom. For children in Grades 1 and up, the evaluation is tied to the levels of achievement described in *The Ontario Curriculum, Grades 1–8: Language* (Ontario Ministry of Education, 1997). The teacher assigns a value (level, mark, comment) that represents the child's achievement of the curriculum expectations, using the reading exemplars and rubrics produced by the Ministry of Education as a guide to ensure consistency. (See *The Ontario Curriculum – Exemplars, Grades 1–8: Reading* [Ontario Ministry of Education, 2000].)

Reporting

Reporting relates to the communication of accurate, comprehensive, and timely information about student achievement to parents, students, and/or other educators. One tool for this is the provincial report card, which students and their families receive three times per year, starting in Grade 1. However, the report card is only one of many ways that teachers can communicate results to children and parents. For Kindergarten children, as with all primary children, reporting should be ongoing and should include a variety of formal and informal methods, ranging from formal written reports and discussions with parents and the child to informal notes to parents and conversations with them. (See the *Guide to the Provincial Report Card* [Ontario Ministry of Education, 1998].)

Reporting provides an opportunity to involve the parents in helping their child to progress as a reader. For reporting to be effective, the teacher must be able to clearly explain the results and next steps. Teachers should discuss specific recommendations for helping the child to reach the provincial standard of level 3. Suggestions might include strategies for individual, classroom, or home-school support.

Teaching Practices

The Framework for Effective Early Reading Instruction (on page 12) lists several practices that support reading achievement in young children. They create the conditions for teachers to provide focused, explicit instruction that addresses the specific needs of individual children and groups of children. These practices are woven throughout the report and include:

- *a balance of direct instruction, guided instruction, independent learning, and practice*

- *large group, small group, and individual instruction, discussion, and collaboration*

- *a variety of assessment and evaluation techniques to inform program planning and instruction*

- *the integration of phonics and word study in reading, writing, and oral language instruction*

- *an uninterrupted literacy block each day*

- *parental and community involvement*

- *high-quality literature and levelled texts*

- *a variety of genres, narratives, informational texts, and electronic media*

- *authentic and motivating literacy experiences and learning activities*

- *interventions for children who are at risk of not learning to read*

- *a supportive classroom culture and environment that promotes higher-order thinking skills*

- *guidance, coaching, and feedback for children*

- *effective classroom organization and management*

4 Help for Children With Reading Difficulties

This report opens with a firm conviction: "A child's success in school and throughout life depends in large part on the ability to read. Educators in Ontario have the profound challenge of making reading a reality for all children."

Many young children experience some kind of difficulty learning to read. For many children, reading difficulties can be identified in Kindergarten or Grade 1 and can be prevented or substantially reduced, but often they are not. Research findings on early reading difficulties are very clear: children who continue to experience difficulties in Grade 3 seldom catch up in later grades. The consequences are well documented. These children are at risk of failing school and dropping out, and they may have limited career opportunities in adulthood. Therefore, it is important to have the conditions and resources – including time, manageable class size, materials, and learning opportunities – that enable teachers to meet the challenges of ensuring that all children learn to read.

The Nature of Reading Difficulties

The foundations of good reading are the same for all children. All readers, regardless of their age, gender, or aptitude, need to develop fluency, comprehension, and the motivation to read in order to become successful readers. Children who experience reading difficulties are no exception. They too must develop the basic foundations for reading, and they require the same types of learning experiences to do so.

Most young children with reading difficulties have problems developing fluency. For these children, identifying words takes a lot of effort. Their reading rate is slow, their word identification is hesitant, and they overrely on contextual cues for word identification. Because most of their cognitive or mental effort is spent trying to identify words, their comprehension suffers. The main prevention and early intervention strategies for these children are effective preparation for literacy and effective classroom instruction.

Preparation for Literacy

Research consistently points to the importance of children beginning their formal reading instruction with the skill and the will that will enable them to learn to read successfully. By the time children begin formal reading instruction, they should have a good understanding of the forms and formats of books and be able to identify and write the letters of the alphabet. They should have basic phonemic awareness, be interested in reading and stories, and see themselves as successful learners *en route* to reading excellence. Some children enter school with such knowledge and attitudes already well developed, but many do not. Participation in developmentally appropriate preschool programs has been shown to improve children's ability to learn to read, especially children from at-risk groups. Kindergarten preparation in literacy is also strongly related to children's success when learning to read. A major step in preventing early reading difficulties is to ensure that an effective Kindergarten reading program is available to all children in Ontario. Such a program provides opportunities for children to listen to stories, poems, and non-fiction materials for enjoyment and information, respond to a variety of materials that are read aloud to them, retell stories in their own words, and demonstrate awareness of written materials, the features of books, and language patterns.

Early Identification and Intervention

Even with effective classroom instruction, some children will need additional supports or interventions. However, teachers should consider supplemental interventions only when effective and adapted instruction has failed to resolve a child's reading difficulties.

Effective intervention requires that teachers recognize as early as possible those children who are experiencing reading difficulties, tailor instruction to address their needs, and provide for supplementary instruction when necessary. If adequate screening and assessment procedures are in place, early intervention may begin even before formal instruction in reading. Interventions that are begun when children are very young have a much better chance of success than interventions begun later.

Interventions begun at Grade 3 are much less likely to succeed than early interventions. It is essential to identify reading difficulties by Grade 1 and to put appropriate supplemental interventions in place immediately. In this way, reading problems can be tackled before they become entrenched and before repeated failures affect children's motivation and compound their difficulties in learning to read and write.

Implementation Process

By Grade 1, all schools should have in place for children a process that allows for the timely implementation of instruction following diagnostic assessment. Once a teacher recognizes that a child is experiencing reading difficulties, the teacher and the child must have access to diagnostic assessment services, specialized interventions, and appropriate instruction. The intensity or duration of the interventions should be based on comprehensive diagnostic assessment. There should be seamless continuity between regular classroom instruction and interventions, and a high degree of cooperation among qualified staff who are serving the same children. The staff should spend the vast majority of their time planning for and delivering instruction directly to children.

Characteristics of Successful Interventions

No one intervention works for all children with reading difficulties. However, interventions that succeed for many children have several characteristics in common. Typically they involve more instructional time for children, but extra time is not enough. Other characteristics include:

- *carefully planned assessments that allow for continual monitoring of the child's response and lead to modifications of the intervention when indicated*

- *teaching methods that are supported by research on how children learn to read and how they should be taught*

- *considerable attention to the materials used (e.g., predictable, patterned, easy-to-more-difficult texts), with a focus on interesting and enjoyable texts at appropriate reading levels*

- *an array of activities (e.g., word study, reading, rereading, and writing)*

Successful interventions generally occur on a daily basis and may occur in focused, short blocks of time, or in longer blocks, with appropriate accommodations in classroom instruction.

Successful interventions are strongly linked with regular classroom instruction, are supported by sound research, reflect an understanding of effective reading instruction (section 3), and are culturally and linguistically appropriate for the individual child. It is critical that interventions be measured against these criteria, and that their effectiveness in helping children with reading difficulties be carefully assessed and monitored.

Children at Risk of Reading Difficulties

Children from certain socio-economic, cultural, or linguistic backgrounds may be more likely statistically to experience reading difficulties. Some researchers refer to these as "at-risk" or "high-risk" groups.

Association with a group that has a statistically higher rate of reading failure has little or nothing to do with a child's *ability* to learn. There are many reasons why classroom instruction may not be meeting the child's needs. For example, many Aboriginal children in remote areas of the province enter school speaking only their first language, and others in urban areas come speaking an English dialect. Instruction may not adequately build upon the literacy, language, and culture that some children bring to school.

In schools where there is a demonstrated high proportion of children who are at risk of reading difficulties, qualified staff and material resources must be available both in the classroom and through support programs. Resources should be distributed equitably to inner city, rural, and remote areas. Efforts in these schools should first focus on supporting the improvement of existing instructional practices, then on implementing additional interventions. In many cases, school-wide efforts at restructuring that integrate organizational issues with coherent, effective classroom instruction have been shown to be more effective than simply adding on new intervention strategies.

It is important for teachers to realize that, with effective instruction, all children can learn to read. It is the school's responsibility to provide for each child the appropriate level of support to reach his or her potential in reading. There must be clear continuity between regular classroom instruction and any interventions provided by support personnel. Interventions will not differ in kind from effective regular classroom instruction, but will differ in frequency, intensity, and focus.

Literacy Teamwork

The classroom teacher should plan appropriate interventions in consultation with other professionals who have expertise in assessment and intervention in reading and related areas (e.g., literacy specialists, speech and language specialists, and audiologists).

Classroom teachers must be given the resources to match their responsibilities. All schools must have appropriate access to a team with specialized expertise in reading intervention.

For French-language schools in some parts of Ontario, and for schools in remote areas, it can be difficult to provide highly specialized service, because the area to be served is so vast. In these situations, technology can be used to link primary teachers to one another (forming a virtual literacy team) and to deliver specialized expertise across long distances to children and teachers. However, it must be noted that the costs for technology solutions are substantially higher in the north than in southern Ontario.

Research findings are clear that, while volunteers may be helpful in implementing supplemental instruction and supports, professionals with the required expertise are essential for the design and delivery of successful interventions. It is the teacher who should teach children how to read.

Professional Development

All teachers in the primary grades need to be well qualified and have opportunities for ongoing professional learning. Teaching reading to young children requires a highly specialized body of knowledge and expertise. The same knowledge and expertise that a teacher uses to help a child who is progressing well in reading will help a child who is struggling. Teachers who are equipped with the broad repertoire of assessment and instructional strategies described earlier in this report are well positioned to identify children with reading difficulties, focus their instruction on individual children's needs, and identify and plan for children whose reading difficulties are severe enough to require specific instruction and support. To stay abreast of new and emerging literacy developments, teachers can consult with local university-based researchers.

So that effective classroom practices that support early identification and intervention might be encouraged, professional development must be available for teachers in Kindergarten to Grade 3 and beyond, with a focus on:

- *maintaining high expectations for children with reading difficulties*

- *understanding the nature of reading difficulties and the impact on achievement*

- *understanding and applying interventions and other modifications*

- *helping children to capitalize on early gains*

Beyond Early Intervention

Effective early identification and intervention will help prevent and significantly decrease reading difficulties for many young children and improve their prospects for school success. However, even exemplary early intervention practices will not guarantee that severe reading difficulties are overcome. Some children will continue to need additional reading instruction and supports to succeed in the later school grades.

As these children grow older and literacy increasingly becomes a vehicle for teaching, learning, and evaluation, instructional and other supports that address their changing needs must be in place.

5 *Target Setting and School Improvement*

The standard that the Province of Ontario sets for reading achievement is the same for all students, regardless of their background, school, or community: to read at level 3 or above in each primary grade. Effective teachers know that different children will need help in different ways to achieve the standard and that, for some, the standard can only be achieved over time. They carefully plan instruction to set challenging but realistic goals, in partnership with the children, parents, and the school literacy team.

Setting targets has been shown to improve the achievement of individuals and whole schools in Canada, the United States, England, and Australia. Target setting leads teachers, administrators, and school boards to become active and vital participants in the improvement process.

Target setting in reading is part of a general strategy of school improvement. The target-setting process begins when teachers and administrators gather and analyse relevant data about children in their school. This analysis enables teachers and the school to identify areas where improvement is needed and to establish meaningful, specific, and realistic goals for future achievement. Targets are a necessary component of the school improvement plan.

Effective schools, where students perform to the best of their abilities, are those that engage in systematic, continuous improvement in the quality of education and that ... have a clear, strong internal focus on issues of instruction, student learning and expectations for teacher and student performance.... [In] a strong 'internal accountability system' ... there is a high degree of alignment among individual teachers about what they can do and about their responsibility for the improvement of student learning.
(Elmore, 2002, pp. 20–21)

Realistic target setting depends on the following:

- **Teamwork across grades.** *The groundwork for reading achievement in Grade 3 and beyond is set in the earliest grades. Schools are more likely to sustain improvement if they promote cross-grade collaboration and a collegial approach.*

- **Effective data management.** *Teachers and school administrators must develop their skills in gathering and analysing student data so that their improvement strategies are based on a correct understanding of student results. This will enable them to make optimal use of all the available information and to identify direct relationships among student performance, classroom instruction, and assessment practices.*

School- and Board-based Assessment

Internal accountability precedes external accountability and is a precondition for any process of improvement. (Elmore, 2002, p. 20)

The primary source of information about student achievement is classroom-based assessment and evaluation. Classroom assessment is described in section 3, in the context of effective reading instruction.

Assessing student work in relation to the achievement charts in *The Ontario Curriculum, Grades 1–8: Language*, 1997 (p. 9) can help teachers, students, and parents better understand what children can already do well and what supports are required to improve their performance. This process encourages teachers and children to reflect, communicate, and work collaboratively in a partnership of learning. It also requires that assessment practices focus on reasoning or thinking skills, the organization of information, the communication of conceptual understandings, and the application of language conventions.

Assessment data have value for individual students, but they can also be used at the school and district levels to:

- *analyse information related to student achievement;*

- *reflect on the overall quality of student learning within the school and the strengths and needs of individuals and groups;*

- *identify areas for improvement and set targets and goals;*

- *plan strategies for achieving the targets that have been set.*

Data can be analysed at one or more of the following levels:

- *at the individual level, by tracking student progress at regular intervals*

- *at the class level, by tracking the class at regular intervals*

- *across classes at the same stage or level of performance*

- *across the primary division at regular intervals*

- *across the school*

- *across the district*

In a whole school approach to reading instruction, teachers make a point of sharing their classroom assessment data so that they can compare classroom practices, adapt strategies, and plan for new resources and professional development, all with the aim of improving student achievement.

In some boards, schools have the benefit of board-wide assessment data, which have been gathered by using board assessment tools or by aggregating the data from teacher tracking records and provincial report cards. As well, some boards have district profiles and school profiles that place data in a geographic and demographic context. These board-wide data can help teachers and schools to analyse their students' progress in relation to schools that have similar or very different characteristics.

Teachers and administrators will recognize that, currently, some schools are more successful in teaching children to read than others. It is important to continue to review one's own school practices to see how they compare with those of more effective schools. Blaming socio-economic or similar factors for low achievement does a disservice to students, teachers, and schools. Research has demonstrated that schools can outperform predictions that are based on the background or prior performance of students. *Schools make a difference*.

Province-wide Assessment

In recent years, province-wide assessments of reading, writing, and mathematics, administered by the Education Quality and Accountability Office (EQAO), have become a source of provincial data to support improvement planning in Ontario education that is focused on school-level and system-wide progress and based on previous performance. Teachers and school principals discuss their school results with parents and the community as part of their effort to work collaboratively to improve results over time for all students, regardless of the school's starting point. EQAO results are taken into account when school improvement plans are developed.

> *The practice of large-scale improvement is the process by which external demands for accountability are translated into concrete structures, processes, norms and instructional practices in schools and school systems. (Elmore, 2002, p. 13)*

Currently some boards and schools use EQAO's Education Quality Indicators Program (EQUIP) and other demographic information to better understand the school context and to locate other schools with similar profiles. This information enables boards and schools to build collaborative networks for sharing improvement plans and instructional strategies, developing materials that address the specific characteristics of their student populations, and finding ways to sustain progress.

In Ontario, EQAO assessment results are used to track trends and patterns of improvement in all schools. Results are also considered when allocation is made of additional provincial funding for resources, professional development, and additional supports to some schools experiencing extraordinary challenges.

Teachers and administrators should be familiar with a variety of valid and reliable reading assessment techniques, including holistic, analytical, and performance-based tools. Provincial assessment provides a snapshot of student performance at the end of the primary division; ongoing assessment provides continuous feedback on student achievement in reading during the early school years.

Ontario school boards, especially the French-language school boards, have come to depend on EQAO for some of their reading assessment needs. Because French-language school boards do not have access to a large variety of reading assessment tools, they focus most of their attention on the EQAO assessment. However, this limits them to an analysis of data from Grade 3 and beyond. Because early diagnosis of reading difficulties is as essential in French as it is in English, it is very important for French school boards to develop a range of diagnostic assessment tools.

Teachers should find evidence of a reasonable alignment between classroom-based assessments and external assessments. If they do not, results should be analysed, so that, where possible, discrepancies can be addressed. EQAO observations and suggestions should be considered during this analysis.

Improvement Planning

The purpose of an accountability system is to focus the resources and capacities of an organization toward a particular end. (Elmore, 2002, p. 23)

EQAO requires that all schools and boards have improvement plans and update their plans annually. Targets for reading, and plans for achieving them, should be part of the overall school improvement plan. Boards and schools should use a breadth of data on reading and set short-term goals for each grade.

The following questions can help principals and teachers to set priorities as they develop or review their school improvement plans:

- *Are all curriculum reading expectations being addressed?*

- *Are all the components of effective reading instruction being implemented in the classroom? (See the Framework for Effective Early Reading Instruction on page 12.)*

- *What types of reading assessment tools and strategies are being used? How often? How is the information about reading assessment tools and strategies being collected at the classroom and school levels?*

- *Are teaching and learning approaches appropriate? Are assessment results used to inform teaching practice on a continuous basis?*

- *Are provincial documents and data from EQAO results being used effectively?*

- *Are children making slower progress in one area than another (e.g., reading comprehension versus fluency)? Are some groups of children making slower progress than others?*

- *How is reading being taught in the content areas (e.g., in social studies, science, or mathematics)?*

- *Are there strategies that could be applied to further motivate at-risk readers to **want** to read?*

- *How are partnerships with parents being developed and maintained so that consistency and support at the school and home levels are provided?*

- *Have all relevant factors been included in the school plan?*

See figure 2 for a list of Key Factors of School Improvement. Principals and teachers can use this as a checklist when developing, reviewing, or revising their school improvement plans.

Figure 2. Key Factors of School Improvement

- **High expectations**
  - Promote attitudes and beliefs that focus on achievement.
  - Set targets for the school, grades, classes, and individual students.
  - Monitor progress towards these targets.
  - Aim for high achievement in later grades by setting intermediate steps in the earlier grades.
  - Encourage students to be independent in their learning.

- **Quality of learning and teaching**
  - Organise limited numbers of groups for effective use of teachers' time.
  - Use direct teaching of groups or classes and structured lessons.
  - Identify clear aims for a block of teaching and share these with students.
  - Match tasks, activities, and resources to achievement levels.
  - Focus on the development of skills and pace of work.
  - Provide opportunities for active learning and questioning and productive homework tasks.

- **Assessment**
  - Ensure good assessment and recording practice, good-quality feedback to students, and clear identification of next steps in learning.
  - Track students' progress, using a range of assessment evidence, in order to identify needs for support and challenge: diagnostic, formative, and summative; holistic and analytical; performance-based.

- **School management**
  - Use "whole-school approaches" led and supported by staff.
  - Identify staff development needs and provide for these.
  - Use cooperative teaching by staff where possible.
  - Monitor classroom practice and implementation of policies.
  - Monitor students' progress across the school and in every class.
  - Provide opportunities for networking and collaborative practice among teachers.
  - Design action plans that are specific, achievable, and relevant.

- **Parental involvement**
  - Provide information about curriculum.
  - Support parents in helping their children's learning.

Note: From *Raising Standards – Setting Targets: Primary Schools Support Pack: Taking a Closer Look at 5–14 Attainment in Primary Schools*, by the Scottish Office, 2000, Edinburgh: Author. Adapted with permission.

6 *Role of the Teacher*

Teachers make a difference in the success of their students when they hold a fundamental belief that all children can learn to read and when they have the skills and determination to make it happen. These teachers base their classroom practices on sound reading theory, provide instruction that meets the specific learning needs of their students, create an organized and stimulating learning environment, and regularly assess their students' reading achievement in relation to the expectations of the Ontario language curriculum. They do not work alone but see themselves as part of a school team committed to ensuring that every child is able to read by the end of Grade 3.

...[E]xcellent reading teachers .... have strong content and pedagogical knowledge, manage classrooms so that there is a high rate of engagement, use strong motivation strategies that encourage independent learning, have high expectations for children's achievement, and help children who are having difficulty. (International Reading Association, 2000, p. 1)

Providing Knowledge and Skills

It is critical that every teacher have an understanding of the complexities of the reading process and the skills to implement all of the components of effective reading instruction. To help children decode and comprehend text in reading, classroom teachers:

- *encourage children to use their prior knowledge, and provide them with appropriate background information if they lack context for understanding text;*

- *provide direct instruction for promoting decoding, fluency, and comprehension;*

- *answer children's questions and monitor performance;*

- *think aloud so that children become aware of how a capable reader and writer approaches literacy tasks;*

- *provide opportunities for children to engage in purposeful talk in the classroom, recognizing that oral language is the foundation for the development of reading and writing skills;*

- *help children ask and answer questions to acquire, clarify, or confirm information and to explore ideas;*

- *recognize the role of higher-order thinking in reading achievement;*

- *reflect on the questions posed by children in order to gain insight into their thinking, identify the nature and the extent of their prior knowledge, and identify gaps in knowledge that need to be addressed in the classroom;*

- *make the link between reading and writing instruction, recognizing that these are interconnected processes and that improvement in one prompts improvement in the other.*

Motivating Children To Read

Teachers have a pivotal role in helping children to develop and maintain a positive attitude towards learning and literacy. Motivated readers read more, use more complex cognitive strategies, and thus become better readers. To motivate children to read, classroom teachers:

- *demonstrate a passion for reading;*

- *act as model readers for their students;*

- *know how children perceive the value of reading, and aim to enhance the perceived value by linking reading with the children's own interests and goals;*

- *know how children perceive their own ability as readers and support them in developing a positive self-image by having them work with texts that are at their current reading level and by providing them with enough time to complete their reading tasks;*

- *encourage children to apply learned reading strategies when they are not sure about the text (e.g., rereading, reading ahead, using pictures, looking at the initial consonant, and asking, "Does it make sense?");*

- *make learning meaningful, taking into account the age, interests, and needs of children;*

- *provide a rich and varied literacy environment that includes interesting reading material, displays, and engaging multimedia resources (e.g., audio, video, and overheads), and that reflects the cultural diversity of the school and community;*

- *provide opportunities for children to choose their own reading material and develop a sense of control over the reading process;*

- *provide opportunities for discussion, teamwork, and other social interactions that make reading interesting and fun;*

- *integrate reading into other activities to show that it is an essential, everyday skill with practical value;*

- *focus on the internal reward of personal satisfaction and the achievement of goals that matter to the individual child.*

Planning and Organizing

Teachers adapt their instruction to match their students' current development in reading, recognizing that as children progress they will need to spend less time developing and practising some skills and more time on others. They use classroom time as effectively as possible, with an appropriate combination of large-group, small-group, and individual instruction. As planners and organizers, they:

- *provide large blocks of uninterrupted classroom time for reading instruction and plenty of meaningful practice;*

- *maintain predictable schedules and classroom routines so that children know what is expected of them in various activities throughout the day;*

- *implement and monitor these established routines before starting small-group instruction, to ensure that children are able to work independently while the teacher is otherwise occupied;*

- *use reflective practice, observation, and a variety of assessment strategies to identify each child's learning needs and provide differentiated instruction;*

- *know strategies and effective practices for engaging children in large groups, small groups, and individual instruction, and for organizing the groups in the most appropriate ways for the learning task (e.g., mixed-ability groupings, or groupings differentiated by age, instructional level, developmental stage, or topic of interest);*

- *use organizational structures and classroom management techniques that enable children to be responsible managers of their own learning time;*

- *monitor the children's time on task and engagement in the task.*

Observing and Assessing

Teachers know that ongoing assessment is fundamentally important for guiding student instruction. They:

- *use a variety of assessment tools and strategies, such as student self-reflection, conferences with students, informal reading inventories, and running records;*

- *use assessment data to determine the current strengths and needs of children;*

- *continually adapt their teaching strategies to match a child's growth;*

- *provide meaningful feedback on the children's work, rather than just providing a mark; celebrate their successes; and let them know where improvements are needed;*

- *pay attention to the needs of children who are at risk of reading failure, and seek timely intervention and supports when it is clear that excellent classroom instruction will not be enough;*

- *work cooperatively with literacy experts who provide reading intervention and supports, in order to ensure that help outside the classroom is supported and reinforced by regular instruction in the classroom.*

Promoting Teamwork

Effective teachers understand the importance of working as part of an early literacy team. They recognize that teachers in the early grades lay the essential groundwork for children to succeed in the higher grades. They know, for example, that children's reading achievement at the end of Grade 3 will depend in large part on the reading instruction they receive in Kindergarten and Grades 1 and 2, and so they work collaboratively to ensure seamless progression.

They meet with colleagues on a regular basis to plan cooperatively, share teaching ideas and strategies, engage in professional reading, and discuss observations based on visits to each others' classrooms. Together they:

- *agree on common literacy strategies;*

- *establish school literacy goals;*

- *build capacity within the primary division.*

As well as working with colleagues, teachers work actively to involve families in their children's learning and encourage reading at home.

Making Cultural Connections

All teachers have a vital role in promoting respect for the cultural diversity of their students and the community. Good teaching builds upon the cultural and language backgrounds, ways of making meaning, and prior knowledge that all children bring to the classroom. Effective teachers:

- *develop their knowledge of other cultures;*

- *have high expectations for all children;*

- *provide a welcoming environment that affirms all children;*

- *work with family members and the community to promote student learning and build bridges of cooperation.*

Culturally informed teaching supports the learning needs of all children, regardless of their cultural or linguistic background. The challenge is not to create the perfect "culturally matched" learning situation for each ethnic group, but to capitalize on diversity and to recognize when an individual child or group of children has a particular need or deficit that is making it harder to learn to read.

> *Teachers' expectations of and relationships with their students profoundly affect students' learning. Numerous research studies in literacy have shown that students are more academically successful when they feel welcomed, valued, and challenged by material that builds upon their prior knowledge, experiences, and interests. When these attitudes, behaviors, and curriculum considerations are missing, children from culturally and linguistically diverse backgrounds may resist learning. (Willis, 2000)*

Teachers in French-language schools have an important additional role in promoting francophone culture and language. They immerse the children in a rich French-language environment that emphasizes the pleasure of speaking and reading in French and promotes *animation culturelle* (cultural development) to ensure that children see the language and culture as relevant and see themselves as active participants in it. As well, they promote community connections by sharing information about francophone arts and services with children and their families.

While the teacher's role in promoting francophone culture is widely accepted, it can be difficult to put this mission into action. It is a huge challenge for teachers to find resources that are adapted to the Franco-Ontarian context and that correspond with *The Kindergarten Program* and the Ontario language curriculum for Grades 1–8. As well, because francophones are widely dispersed throughout the province, it is difficult for them to work together to create new resources and share existing resources. But in spite of these challenges – and even more *because* of them – it is vital that teachers include themes favouring the development of cultural life in French.

Pursuing Professional Expertise

[Professional development] must move beyond the 'sit and get' model of one-shot workshops, conferences, in-service days, and graduate courses that have no connection with the real work of schools. [It] should be ongoing, intensive, and an integral part of a teacher's regular workday. ... In addition, professional development should demonstrate a positive correlation with increased teacher effectiveness and improved student achievement. (US Department of Education, 1996)

Teachers who are committed to excellence in reading instruction recognize that there is no single instructional program or method that is effective for all children. This is why they understand the importance of improving their professional knowledge individually and within a team, and view themselves as lifelong, reflective learners. They seek out opportunities to expand their knowledge by participating in peer coaching, mentorships, professional reading circles, networking opportunities with colleagues, and literacy workshops and conferences.

Most effective professional development happens in schools during the school day, with the support and involvement of an onsite lead literacy teacher. It is research-based, practical, ongoing, and tied in a clear and meaningful way to the expectations in the Ontario curriculum and to the goal of improving student achievement. Topics could include: phonemic awareness and concepts about print; phonics and word study; vocabulary development; selection and use of high-quality literature to develop and expand oral language and vocabulary; text comprehension; written expression; ongoing assessment to inform instruction; and strategies for motivating children to read and write.

Focused professional development affirms for teachers that they have a central role to play in student learning, and shows them how to be successful in that role. It respects and nurtures the teachers' intellectual and leadership capacity. It encourages teachers to develop the daily habit of asking good questions of themselves and others, reflecting on their practices, and striving to improve both individually and as a team.

7 *Supportive Leadership*

There can be no more important goal for educators in Ontario elementary schools than to ensure that all children become effective readers who can apply their skills to build new knowledge. To achieve this goal, teachers, principals, central support staff, and superintendents must rededicate their efforts to build strong relationships, and must continually strive to improve

> *Leadership is about learning that leads to constructive change. (Lambert, 1998, p. 5)*

their capacity to provide excellent instruction for children. The real measure of success is student achievement in reading: in effective schools and boards, student assessment data are used on an ongoing basis to monitor progress and guide the school in improvement planning.

Teamwork within and among schools is essential. Strong relationships among teachers enhance their opportunities for sharing effective practices and increase their personal and professional competence. Strong relationships, within and among schools, help to ensure that programs support each other and optimize opportunities for increasing literacy.

Supporting Professional Development

All contributors – teachers, teacher librarians, principals, support staff, and superintendents – need to focus on understanding the goals and key strategies for reading instruction so that the school continues to strengthen its capacity to improve. Classroom teachers can strive to increase their skills, but they cannot succeed in isolation. They need the support of other teachers, including the lead literacy teacher, as well as the principal, central support staff, and superintendent. Planned and sustained professional development is the key.

Successful professional development has these characteristics:

People

- *Everyone who affects student learning, including the principal, is involved and participates as part of the learning team.*

- *Each member of the learning team has an individual professional development plan for reading, and engages in ongoing self-evaluation.*

- *Experts contribute from both inside and outside the district.*

- *Strong instructional leadership is provided by the school's lead teacher and principal, and by board literacy specialists, superintendents, and the director of education.*

- *An integral goal is teacher self-efficacy – the firm conviction within teachers that they can make a difference in their students' reading achievement, and that they have the knowledge and skills to do it.*

Context

- *The content reflects the best available research and is aligned with* The Kindergarten Program *and the Ontario language curriculum for Grades 1 to 8.*

- *Adequate time is allocated for developing professional expertise during school hours.*

- *The commitment is long-term and is supported by adequate funding.*

- *Learning is tied to school improvement.*

- *Change occurs in definable steps.*

Processes

- *A variety of professional learning activities are offered at the school, at the system level, and beyond, based on need.*

- *Learning is reinforced through a cycle of theory, demonstration, practice, feedback, and coaching.*

- *Follow-up is provided after concentrated professional development.*

- *Evaluation of the professional development is based ultimately on its impact on teacher effectiveness and student learning.*

Role of the Principal

Effective principals are committed curriculum leaders who are dedicated to making literacy a school priority. By sharing or distributing leadership, they build support for the school literacy plan and build the capacity to achieve its goals. They pay special attention to finding and developing in-school leaders, such as the lead literacy teacher, and to consolidating and extending the leadership skills of experienced teachers so that they can support their colleagues. One of the responsibilities of the principal in a French language school is to ensure that teachers are offered appropriate professional development that will allow them to include *animation culturelle* (cultural development) as a component of their program.

Effective leadership in literacy involves identifying important literacy goals and enabling teachers to achieve those goals through supervision and support. The principal has a direct impact on teaching and learning by:

- *sharing leadership*

- *promoting learning teams*

- *optimizing school and classroom timetables*

- *supporting classroom instruction*

- *setting targets that improve student achievement*

- *developing the school literacy plan*

- *promoting home/school/community partnerships*

- *providing interventions and supports*

Sharing Leadership

A whole school approach to literacy, based on a philosophy of distributed leadership, provides classroom and specialist teachers with opportunities to assume leadership roles in curriculum and instruction. This model also gives teachers responsibility for thinking about individual and collective strategies for working more efficiently and effectively with children, with the key goal of improving the reading skills of all children.

The role of the principal in shared leadership is to:

- *foster an atmosphere of trust;*

- *identify teachers who have exemplary practices;*

- *coach/mentor teachers so that they develop their leadership skills;*

- *provide opportunities for teachers to share knowledge with each other;*

- *involve teachers in sharing with each other;*

- *form professional learning teams focused on literacy instruction and assessment;*

- *engage teachers in school planning at different stages (e.g., collecting data, setting goals, monitoring progress, and providing feedback);*

- *accept accountability for student achievement and foster support of the vision and the goals of the school plan;*

- *embrace opportunities to learn with teachers about effective practice;*

- *act as an instructional leader, providing guidance and leadership;*

- *understand that teachers responsible for libraries have a pivotal role in early literacy development.*

Promoting Learning Teams

Professional development is most powerful when teachers learn and work together as a team and pursue clearly articulated school-based goals for literacy. Principals should work closely with teachers to develop a plan for ongoing learning, addressing current literacy issues identified by teachers and by research into effective practice.

The role of the principal in promoting learning teams is to:

- *establish a literacy team in the primary division;*

- *communicate and collaborate at regularly scheduled times with the primary division and grade teams;*

- *collaborate with team members to set the agenda for literacy meetings and discuss topics relevant to best practices in reading instruction;*

- *ensure that professional development is relevant by linking it with school literacy priorities and assessment data;*

- *ensure that professional development leads to improvements in the classroom by providing monitoring and feedback;*

- *provide time for teachers to learn together;*

- *provide opportunities for teachers to be trained in coaching and mentoring, as well as opportunities for them to practise these skills.*

Optimizing School and Classroom Timetables

Research on effective schools shows that schools and classrooms should be organized around the learning needs of students so that meaningful and sustainable improvements in student achievement can be supported. To help maximize instructional time and engage students in learning, the principal should:

- *schedule large uninterrupted blocks of time for reading and literacy instruction;*

- *explore alternative timetables and school organizations that maximize instructional time;*

- *reduce or eliminate unnecessary interruptions during instructional time;*

- *schedule time for team planning and learning;*

- *ensure that children who are at risk of not learning to read have optimal access to interventions at appropriate times during the school day;*

- *talk with teachers about monitoring their students' time on task.*

Supporting Classroom Instruction

Effective reading instruction involves children in a range of reading contexts that can be adjusted to meet the needs of children at different levels of achievement and with different interests. The role of the principal in effective reading instruction is to:

- *understand the reading process and be able to articulate it to teachers and parents;*

- *be knowledgeable about the components of effective reading instruction and the framework necessary for supporting it (see the Framework for Effective Early Reading Instruction on page 12);*

- *review individual classroom timetables to ensure that they provide effective literacy blocks;*

- *value teaching that builds on the cultural backgrounds and first languages of the children;*

- *visit classrooms to observe reading instruction;*

- *monitor teachers' reading programs to ensure that the components are effectively implemented and observable in classrooms (e.g., the effective use of levelled texts, guided reading, and word walls);*

- *establish budgets that give priority to reading and allow for classroom resources, time for teamwork, professional development, and materials for the classrooms;*

- *ensure that reading resources are available and accessible to all.*

Setting Targets That Improve Student Achievement

High expectations for student achievement need to be clearly articulated to teachers and parents. The role of the principal is to:

- *collaborate with teachers to establish targets for student achievement in reading based on results from a variety of assessment tools;*

- *participate in the board-wide target setting and reporting that is required by the Ministry of Education;*

- *establish a vision in the school that reflects an expectation of high achievement for all children;*

- *regularly review the school improvement plan and targets for reading achievement with staff and the school council.*

Developing the School Literacy Plan

Every school improvement plan should include an EQAO plan and a comprehensive literacy plan. The literacy plan guides instruction for promoting student achievement, improves teachers' skills, and promotes community involvement in early literacy. The role of the principal in this process is to:

- *guide the school improvement planning team in reviewing student performance in literacy;*

- *engage teachers in establishing goals and setting priorities based on a variety of assessment data;*

- *work with teachers to interpret data on student achievement;*

- *use consistent assessment tools from year to year, and within the year at specific points;*

- *connect professional development with the goals of the school literacy plan;*

- *ensure that teachers use high-quality assessment tools in their day-to-day practice to inform their teaching;*

- *regularly review goals and priorities to measure progress and make necessary adjustments for improvement;*

- *align school budget priorities with goals in the literacy plan;*

- *ensure that literacy remains a priority in the everyday operations of the school;*

- *celebrate both incremental and significant achievements in student and staff literacy learning;*

- *align plans with the Ontario Ministry of Education's* The Kindergarten Program, *1998;* The Ontario Curriculum, Grades 1–8: Language, *1997; exemplar documents; and board policies and directives.*

Promoting Home/School/Community Partnerships

Children make significantly greater progress when their parents, caregivers, and the community work together with the school to encourage their reading achievement. The role of the principal is to:

- *work with the school council in fulfilling its mandate to support student achievement;*

- *encourage parents and caregivers to support their child's learning in meaningful ways (e.g., through family reading, letter writing, and storytelling);*

- *establish processes for communicating the reading expectations to parents;*

- *affirm the ongoing development of the children's first language in the home;*

- *make links with community agencies that offer literacy services;*

- *provide parents and caregivers with access to reading material that their children can use at home;*

- *seek meaningful partnerships with high schools, community colleges, and universities.*

For principals in the French-language system, the responsibility for promoting home and community partnerships has an added dimension. While respecting the cultural diversity of students and the first language of the home, they need to participate in ensuring the continued vitality of Franco-Ontarian culture. This means that they have an obligation to encourage families both to use French in the home as much as possible and to actively seek out French-language experiences for their children. Principals must also plan stimulating cultural activities throughout the school to reach and connect with children of all grades, giving life to the language and enabling children to live as francophones. Modes for cultural enrichment might include school newspapers, radio, sports, arts events, and after-school programs.

Providing Interventions and Supports

Schools that are effective in teaching early literacy recognize the need for short-term, research-based interventions that address the specific needs or gaps of "at-risk" learners. The role of the principal in providing interventions and supports is to:

- *ensure that interventions are based on student needs, aligned with the classroom reading instructional practices, and delivered by a trained literacy expert;*

- *monitor the assessment strategies used to determine the students' level of achievement;*

- *organize timetables so that remedial help is given at appropriate times and in appropriate settings during the school day;*

- *monitor the progress of children in special programs who are at risk of not learning to read;*

- *monitor the development and implementation of Individual Education Plans (IEPs) related to reading instruction.*

Role of the Lead Literacy Teacher

Every school in Ontario with a primary division should have a lead literacy teacher who has extensive expertise in reading instruction and staff development. The lead literacy teacher's main goal is to improve reading achievement by working collaboratively with teachers to deepen their understanding of the reading process and extend their repertoire of instructional strategies. Lead teachers support principals in ensuring effective reading instruction throughout the school.

To be effective, lead literacy teachers should have a thorough conceptual understanding about the reading and writing process, about how children and adults learn, and about how to create opportunities for them to learn effectively. Lead literacy teachers must have a clear and well-articulated vision of what is possible in student achievement in reading.

If lead teachers are to fulfil their unique and pivotal role, their classroom responsibilities must take into account the time needed within the school day to model lessons and collaborate with and mentor other staff.

Effective lead literacy teachers have the following knowledge and skills:

- *extensive knowledge of effective reading practice*

- *the ability to evaluate and interpret current research*

- *in-depth knowledge of how children learn to read and write*

- *expertise in assessment as it relates to the reading process*

- *commitment to student improvement*

- *successful experience in primary teaching*

- *demonstrated knowledge of the principles of adult learning*

- *strong commitment to teamwork*

- *strong interpersonal skills*

The main responsibilities for lead literacy teachers include:

- *observing, coaching, and mentoring other teachers*

- *promoting learning teams*

- *managing resources*

- *analysing and interpreting student achievement data*

Observing, Coaching, and Mentoring

Lead teachers help their team members to refine their instructional strategies by observing, coaching, and mentoring them in the classroom. The role of the lead teacher is to:

- *model effective instructional strategies;*

- *work with the principal and teachers to schedule the literacy block;*

- *help teachers to reflect on their practice;*

- *help teachers to establish routines that allow for effective literacy instruction;*

- *model how to use professional resources to improve instructional strategies;*

- *help teachers to make meaningful connections between reading theory and classroom practice;*

- *work with new teachers and their mentors to establish a classroom reading program.*

Promoting Learning Teams

The lead literacy teacher supports the primary division learning team in its ongoing development. The role of the lead teacher in professional development is to:

- *consult with teachers on topics for ongoing learning;*

- *lead professional training sessions in areas determined by the priorities and goals in the school literacy plan;*

- *lead discussions among teachers on current reading practices and current reading research;*

- *provide opportunities for teachers to share their own effective practices with each other;*

- *work collaboratively with principals and other lead teachers in the board to develop and share effective practices;*

- *engage in ongoing professional learning and self-reflection;*

- *support the principal in scheduling regular in-school literacy meetings.*

Managing Resources

Books, tapes, and other learning materials are essential resources for early reading instruction. Time and attention need to be given to selecting, maintaining, and distributing these resources. The role of the lead teacher is to:

- *share appropriate professional resources with teachers;*

- *establish a framework or process for tracking early literacy resources in the school;*

- *instruct teachers on how to use levelled materials;*

- *work with classroom teachers and the teacher-librarian to establish resource priorities.*

Analysing and Interpreting Student Achievement Data

The ability to assess literacy is the foundation for systematically improving student achievement in reading. To help their teams develop this ability, lead teachers:

- *model how to use assessment tools effectively;*

- *support teachers in assessing student reading achievement at specific points during the school year;*

- *model how to use student achievement data to plan for instruction;*

- *work with the principal to analyse student achievement data;*

- *work with the principal to interpret aggregate data from classroom assessments in reading for Kindergarten to Grade 3;*

- *participate in developing and revising the school literacy plan as part of school improvement planning.*

Role of the Superintendent

> Leadership is the guidance and direction of instructional improvement.... Distributed leadership does not mean that no one is responsible for overall performance of the organization. It means, rather, that the job of administrative leaders is primarily about enhancing the skills and knowledge of people in the organization, creating a common culture of expectations around the use of those skills and knowledge, holding the various pieces of the organization together in a productive relationship with each other, and holding individuals accountable for their contributions to the collective results. (Elmore 2000, pp. 13, 15)

Success in reading must be a concrete goal, which results in tangible actions by teachers, principals, and superintendents. Effective superintendents assume responsibility for increasing student achievement in reading in their district and sustain this improvement by promoting shared or distributed leadership for literacy.

The superintendent has a dual responsibility: to supervise the development and implementation of the district improvement plan and to ensure that principals have developed and implemented the literacy component of the school improvement plan.

Effective leadership by superintendents in the area of literacy addresses the following areas:

- *creating vision and focus*

- *building leadership*

- *setting targets that improve student achievement*

- *managing resources*

Creating Vision and Focus

A key role of the superintendent is to actively articulate a vision of high achievement in reading to the board, principals, teachers, and parents. This vision establishes a clear purpose as well as the standard for achievement. A shared sense of purpose leads to shared action. The role of the superintendent as visionary is to:

- *facilitate a system-wide commitment to early literacy;*

- *establish policies that support effective literacy instruction;*

- *help principals to recognize and articulate what their schools must accomplish in the area of reading instruction and student achievement;*

- *create a climate of accountability for improvement in reading results;*

- *build strong professional development networks at the board level;*

- *establish a focus on reading at the local level;*

- *ensure that reading initiatives are aligned at the provincial, board, school, and classroom levels;*

- *manage the implementation of new initiatives so that schools maintain a focus on early reading;*

- *engage the expertise and leadership of central support staff.*

Building Leadership

For innovation to succeed, an organization must strengthen its leadership capacity. Effective superintendents do this primarily by creating professional learning teams of principals, focusing on reading instruction and literacy leadership.

The role of the superintendent in building leadership capacity is to:

- *provide central support staff that can help schools build their literacy teams;*

- *advise principals about board and ministry policies and documents related to reading;*

- *support principals, teachers, and central support staff in implementing new reading strategies;*

- *facilitate a shared culture for learning in communities of schools;*

- *ensure that literacy is a primary consideration in staffing decisions and give schools the opportunity to hire leaders in reading or literacy;*

- *build groups of teachers at a system level who have acquired strong instructional knowledge in reading, as well as skills in coaching or mentoring;*

- *assess the instructional leadership capacity of principals;*

- *include a reading component in every meeting of principals, to enhance their understanding of effective classroom practices;*

- *form professional learning teams focused on leadership for literacy;*

- *mentor new principals in the development of a school literacy plan;*

- *provide principals with research that helps them to carry out their work more effectively;*

- *encourage and facilitate professional development in key areas (e.g., reading instruction, leadership for literacy, team building);*

- *recognize and celebrate both small and large changes in student achievement in literacy within schools.*

Setting Targets That Improve Student Achievement

Superintendents can help to establish clear and measurable goals for achievement, can use these goals and assessment tools to monitor progress, and can help principals to take appropriate action. The role of the superintendent in this is to:

- *systematically monitor progress in reading at each school by examining school-based assessments, system-wide assessments, and external assessments (such as the province-wide EQAO results);*

- *consult with principals to set reasonable targets for reading levels;*

- *share current assessment tools that are being used in reading;*

- *review school plans in literacy with each principal or team of principals;*

- *create opportunities for principals to problem-solve issues affecting student achievement in their schools;*

- *provide leadership in using data for continuous school improvement and monitor the effects of school improvement planning.*

Managing Resources

Effective resource allocation reflects a decision-making process based on student needs and thoughtfully articulated action plans. The role of the superintendent is to:

- *supervise the acquisition and development of resources to support student achievement in reading;*

- *provide appropriate support for schools with unique needs;*

- *allocate financial resources according to priorities that have been identified at the board level;*

- *allocate funds to support success in school-based projects;*

- *monitor the use of funds allocated to school-based projects.*

8 Home and Community Connections

Effective schools do not exist in isolation; they are an integral part of the communities they serve. Effective schools and classroom teachers involve families in their children's education and help them to connect with relevant resources in the broader community. They also work in partnership with community groups, service agencies, and postsecondary institutions to expand their knowledge, skills, and resources for helping all children learn to read.

Family involvement in a child's education is a more important factor in student success than family income or education. (International Reading Association, 2002, p. 2)

Communities, in turn, have a vested interest in promoting reading skills because the personal and social benefits of literacy are so great, and the costs of illiteracy are so high. Children who do not learn to read in school are far more likely to require expensive and ongoing community support than children who become successful readers.

Parental Involvement

Parental involvement is a key element in a school's plan to make every child a successful reader. While the school has primary responsibility for formal reading instruction, children are more likely to succeed when their parents are actively involved in their education.

Parents need to know that children learn to read in a series of developmental stages that lead over time to independent reading. The booklet *Helping Your Child Learn to Read: A Parent's Guide* (Ontario Ministry of Education, 2001) is a practical resource for helping parents to understand the developmental stages. It describes the characteristics of the beginning reader, the emergent reader, the early reader, and the fluent reader. It also offers tips for helping children learn to read. Teachers can help parents by describing the most appropriate home activities at each stage in a child's reading development.

The best time for children to start learning to read is when they are very young. The National Longitudinal Survey of Children and Youth[3] has found that children who had been read to several times a day at the age of two to three years did substantially better in kindergarten than those whose parents did not read as often. The same study found

---

3. The National Longitudinal Survey of Children and Youth (NLSCY) is a long-term study of Canadian children that follows their development and well-being from birth to early adulthood. The NLSCY began in 1994 and is jointly conducted by Statistics Canada and Human Resources Development Canada. See, for example, Lipps and Yiptong-Avila, 1999, pp. 5–6.

that children who experienced a stimulating preschool environment had significantly higher scores on standardized vocabulary measures.

Reading in the Home Language

Parents of children whose first language is not the language of instruction should be encouraged to continue to develop their children's literacy skills in the home language. Skills in a first language naturally support and reinforce the learning of a second language.

It can be extremely difficult, however, for children in the French-language system whose first language is not French to receive immersion in the language outside of school and become fluent speakers and readers. Without this fluency, children risk falling behind in all school subjects. In these cases, parents should work with the children to provide as much exposure to the French language as possible and should encourage the use of French at home.

Parents in the Classroom

Parents and other family members who are able to volunteer in the classroom can provide valuable support for the classroom reading program. For example, they can read aloud to children, help them with homework, and practise sight words and letter recognition. For children whose home language is not the language of instruction, parent volunteers who speak the same language can help to ease the transition into school.

Schools have a responsibility to provide appropriate training and support to enable parent volunteers to make a meaningful contribution. However, parent volunteers cannot be expected to be reading experts. Children who are experiencing serious reading difficulties should be helped by professionals who are highly trained in reading instruction.

Encouraging Family Involvement

It is important for teachers and administrators to identify parents' level of participation and then work towards removing barriers that may be preventing further participation. When teachers are supportive, responsive, and welcoming, they encourage parents to be positive partners in their child's education. Teachers can help to build positive partnerships with families by:

- *working respectfully with families and communicating effectively with them;*

- *showing a genuine interest in the children;*

- *responding promptly and constructively to parent concerns;*

- *promoting a philosophy of teamwork;*

- *being sensitive to the needs of parents and families;*

- *developing and promoting multicultural understanding;*

- *using creative problem-solving strategies.*

These are some practical ways that teachers can help families to support early reading achievement:

- *Share information about family activities that promote reading, such as completing homework, reading in the place of worship, following daily living routines, reading signs, and writing lists and personal messages.*

- *Provide families with books and book lists. The availability of books for children varies from home to home, regardless of socio-economic status. Schools can encourage reading at home by sending home familiar materials to develop fluency. This is particularly important for the Franco-Ontarian community, where books in French may only be available at schools.*

- *Explain the strategies that children use to decode and understand text. During the reporting conference, the teacher can provide the parents with prompts (e.g.: "Look at the first letter in the word," "What makes sense?") to move the child through the text.*

The overall goal of reading at home is to motivate further reading and to provide an opportunity for parents and children to engage in a positive learning experience together.

Cultural Enrichment and Support

Cultural awareness and respect for diversity are fundamental to a healthy, vibrant society. It is important to value the variety of contexts in which our children live. The more culturally enriched the children's environment is, the more background knowledge they will acquire to help them understand and interpret the wide range of stories and information they will encounter through reading at school. Efforts to welcome, understand, and affirm all children – and to treat their cultural and linguistic backgrounds as equally valid and important – should be reflected in every facet of the school and classroom environment.

Libraries, theatre groups, play groups, day-care centres, and community centres may already have programs in place that enrich the background knowledge and skills of young children and stimulate their motivation to read, or they may be willing to forge partnerships with local schools to develop appropriate programs. Cultural groups in the community can also be encouraged to contribute books, audiotapes, and videos for classroom libraries or for home-lending programs, or to participate in intergenerational projects. Schools can help families to become aware of local language and cultural resources by creating community directories and promoting services and special events in newsletters and on school bulletin boards and websites. Pen pal programs, student exchanges, and Internet connections can extend the sense of community beyond the local neighbourhood and into the wider world.

The Francophone Context

The francophone community faces a greater challenge because these social and cultural resources may not be readily available or even exist. The difficulty lies in the fact that the francophone population is scattered over a large territory – a dispersion that results, in some cases, in very small communities that cannot sustain French-language libraries, theatre, singing groups, day care, community centres, and other services. Social and cultural connections such as these are critical for the French-language system and, in many cases, schools must act as a driving force to provide them or ensure they are in place.

French-language schools have the important responsibility to maintain and promote francophone culture and language in a largely English-speaking society. In some communities, the school is the only milieu where the language is spoken, where books in French are available, and where cultural activities take place. In addition to being a teaching and learning environment, the school becomes a community centre.

Reading instruction – in fact, all of school life – should immerse the children and their families in a rich French-language environment that emphasizes the pleasure of speaking and reading in French and promotes *animation culturelle* (cultural development) to ensure that children see the language and culture as alive and relevant.

Community Agencies

Community agencies can connect the family with community supports that will help to prepare the child and family for reading in the school years. The school, in turn, is often the gateway to community support. Community agencies and schools must coordinate their efforts in order to have the most positive impact on the children and families that they serve. Early identification of children who are at risk of not learning to read can alert the school to be prepared for special needs and can help to ensure that the right instruction is in place when the child enters school. Together, the school and community agencies can strategize about ways to ease the transition to school for all children in their care, and especially for those who are at risk of learning difficulties.

Universities

Elementary schools and postsecondary institutions make natural partners in the pursuit of excellence in education. The school-university connection is reciprocal and interdependent. Such partnerships can and do provide opportunities for putting theory and research into practice, and practice into research. Schools and teachers play an essential role in the education of future teachers when they partner with Faculties of Education to supervise teacher candidates during their field placements. Faculties of Education are vitally important to schools because they educate future teachers and school administrators and are essential partners in continuing teacher education and ongoing learning. Universities, and Faculties of Education in particular, conduct research on how children learn to read and how they should be taught. Findings from this and related research (e.g., on educational leadership) form part of the evidence base that informs classroom practices and school improvement planning in early reading. Active collaboration between schools and universities – regarding pre-service, graduate and continuing education, and research – can be mutually beneficial. It should be a defining feature of the Ontario context for the teaching and learning of early reading.

9 *Conclusion*

The goal of Ontario's Early Reading Strategy is to raise the level of reading achievement in Ontario classrooms. The strategy focuses on the reading skills of children from Junior Kindergarten to Grade 3. Research indicates that a solid foundation in reading is essential for future learning in school, and that schools can improve student achievement in later grades by improving reading skills in the early years.

The Ministry of Education convened the Early Reading Panel to advise teachers, principals, and educational leaders on ways to ensure that students of whatever background or aptitude become effective readers. The panel concluded that the key to accomplishing this challenging but achievable goal is focused and effective classroom instruction delivered by skilled and motivated teachers.

Good teaching does not happen in isolation. Teachers have the greatest long-term impact on their students when they work together with their fellow teachers, resource staff, school administrators, and the school board to set and achieve goals for their students, and when they involve parents and other community partners in the learning process.

This report is one important component of the Ontario Early Reading Strategy. Other components based on this report include a technical guide detailing practical applications for classroom instruction, e-learning modules for online learning for all JK–Grade 3 teachers and for administrators, as well as training for lead teachers and principals.

The time is right to consolidate the lessons learned from the convergence of research and classroom practice into a consistent framework for reading instruction that will raise the overall level of reading achievement in Ontario schools. For the sake of all children, the time for reading is now.

Glossary

achievement levels

Four possible levels of student achievement, as defined in the Ontario curriculum for each grade. Level 3, which is the "provincial standard", indicates a high level of achievement, or between B– and B+. Parents of students who are achieving at level 3 can be confident that their children are on track for the next grade. Levels 1 and 2 identify achievement that falls below the provincial standard. Level 4 identifies achievement that surpasses the standard.

ALF

Actualisation linguistique du français. A program for students who have a right to a French-language education, but who have little or no knowledge of French. Most ALF students speak English as a first language. (*Also see* **PDF.**)

animation culturelle

A philosophy and program to support student achievement in French-language schools by providing students with meaningful learning opportunities in French and a nurturing French-language environment that fosters the development of strong French-language skills and promotes a francophone cultural identity.

assessment

A process of gathering, recording, and analysing information about a child's knowledge and skills from a variety of sources and, where appropriate, providing descriptive feedback to guide the child's improvement. (*Also see* **evaluation**.)

at risk

Used in this document to mean students who may not meet the curriculum expectations for reading at their age or grade level.

Bloom's taxonomy

A widely used way of classifying educational objectives, developed in the 1950s by a group of researchers headed by Benjamin Bloom of the University of Chicago. It describes thinking skills as a hierarchy, with knowledge and memory as the entry point, followed progressively by comprehension, application, analysis, synthesis, and evaluation.

cloze procedure

In a cloze procedure the teacher produces a text in which some words have been deleted, and students attempt to insert suitable words. This technique is used to check the difficulty of a text or type of text, and to identify whether students will be able to read the text independently or will require instructional support.

comprehension

The ability to draw meaning from spoken and written words.

comprehension strategies

Conscious plans that readers use to make sense of the text (e.g., by asking questions such as: "How does this connect with what I already know? What pictures does this text create in my mind? How can I say this in my own words?").

concepts about print

Awareness about how language is conveyed in print. These concepts include knowing and understanding the following: directionality (reading left to right, top to bottom); differences between letters and words (words are made of letters; there are spaces between words); capitalization; spelling patterns; punctuation; and common characteristics of books (title, author, front/back).

dialect

A variant of a language that may involve pronunciation, grammar, or vocabulary that differs from the standard form of the language. Dialects are governed by rules, but the rules are different from those governing the standard form of a language.

decoding

In reading, the ability to sound out letters and words.

distributed leadership

An approach to sharing leadership among team members. In distributed leadership, team members share responsibility and authority, guided by a common vision or goal. A key role of the senior administrator is to involve the team in defining the shared vision, enable team members to develop their knowledge and skills, promote productive relationships among team members, and hold individuals accountable for their contributions to the collective effort. In this document, distributed leadership is also called "shared leadership".

ELD

English literacy development. Instruction for students who speak a variation of English that differs from standard English, and who need help to improve their skills in reading, writing, and oral communication. (*Also see* **ESL**. *For the comparable French-language program, see* **PDF**.)

emergent literacy

An early stage of literacy development in young children, characterized by a growing awareness of, and interest in, books and writing. Emergent readers and writers may, for example, "read" a book from memory, or "write" a message using scribbles, pictures, or approximations of letters. Children are most likely to demonstrate emergent literacy behaviours if others read to them, encourage them to talk about stories and events, and provide them with opportunities to explore books on their own.

environmental print

Words and symbols encountered outside of books in everyday life (e.g., product labels, logos, and traffic signs).

EQAO

Education Quality and Accountability Office. An independent agency of the Ontario government that designs and implements a province-wide program of student assessment within government-established parameters. It reports to the Minister of Education, the public, and the education community on assessment and education issues, and makes recommendations for improvement.

EQUIP

Education Quality Indicators Program. A source of demographic and other environmental information to help teachers and administrators in their joint planning for school improvement. EQUIP data provide a context for examining and understanding student achievement scores. The program is operated by EQAO.

ESL

English as a second language. Instruction for students who have little or no fluency in English, designed to help them build their English-language proficiency. (*Also see* **ELD**. *For the comparable French-language program, see* **ALF**.)

evaluation

A value judgement about the quality of a student's work at a point in time. (*Also see* **assessment**.)

exemplars

Samples of student work that demonstrate a particular level of achievement. (*See* Ontario Ministry of Education, *The Ontario Curriculum – Exemplars, Grades 1–8: Reading,* 2000.)

expectations

Statements in the Ontario curriculum about the knowledge and skills that students are expected to learn and demonstrate in their class work and in the activities used to assess their achievement.

fluency

The ability to identify words accurately and read text quickly; the ability to read text aloud with good expression.

grapheme

The smallest part of *written* language that represents a phoneme in the spelling of a word. A grapheme may be just one letter, such as *b, d, f, p, s*; or several letters, such as *ch, sh, th, -ck, ea, -igh*.

graphophonic cues

Visual information on the page, based on sound-symbol correspondences, that helps readers to decode text. Graphophonic cues occur within words and may include letter or sound relationships, word patterns, and words recognized by sight.

guided reading

A method of instruction in which the teacher works with a small group of students who have similar reading processes. The group composition changes as a result of teacher observation and assessment. The teacher selects the students, introduces them to a new book, and supports them through it.

IEP

See **Individual Education Plan**.

independent reading

A method of instruction in which students select familiar and unfamiliar texts to read by themselves or with a partner.

Individual Education Plan (IEP)

A plan that identifies a student's specific learning expectations and outlines how the school will address these expectations through appropriate special education programs and services. It also identifies the methods by which the student's progress will be reviewed.

intervention

For a student with special needs, targeted supportive instruction that follows diagnostic assessment.

lead literacy teacher

A teacher with extensive expertise in reading instruction and staff development. The lead literacy teacher's main goal is to improve reading achievement by working collaboratively with teachers to deepen their understanding of the reading process and extend their repertoire of instructional strategies. Lead teachers support principals in ensuring effective reading instruction throughout the school.

letter formation

The ability to print or write letters.

letter recognition

The ability to name a letter that is displayed, or find a letter in a group.

levelled texts

Reading material that has been sorted according to level of difficulty so that children and teachers can select texts at the child's current instructional reading level.

metacognition

Having knowledge (cognition) and being able to understand it, have control over it, and make appropriate use of it. In short, being able to think about the thinking process and how to develop or improve it.

miscue analysis

A diagnostic technique in which a student reads a passage aloud and the teacher marks miscues on a copy of the passage, or tallies the errors. The results are then analysed by the teacher to plan instruction.

PDF

Perfectionnement du français. A program designed for students who speak a regional variation of French that is very different from standard French. These students are recent arrivals from other countries. Their schooling thus far has either been very different from the schooling in Franco-Ontarian schools, or has been disrupted. These students lack rudimentary skills in reading, writing, and mathematics. PDF also familiarizes the students with the Franco-Ontarian education system and with their new social and cultural environment. (*Also see* **ALF**. *For the comparable English-language program, see* **ELD**.)

phoneme

The smallest part of *spoken* language that makes a difference in the meaning of words. English has about 44 phonemes. A few words, such as *a* or *oh*, have only one phoneme. Most words, however, have more than one phoneme. The word *if* has two phonemes (/i/ /f/); *check* has three phonemes (/ch/ /e/ /k/); and *stop* has four phonemes (/s/ /t/ /o/ /p/). Sometimes one phoneme is represented by more than one letter.

phonemic awareness

The ability to hear, identify, and manipulate the individual sounds (phonemes) in spoken words.

phonics

Instruction that teaches children the relationships between the letters (graphemes) of written language and the individual sounds (phonemes) of spoken language.

phonological awareness

A broad term that includes phonemic awareness. In addition to phonemes, phonological awareness activities can involve work with rhymes, words, syllables, and onsets of rimes.

picture cues

Story illustrations that are closely matched to the text so that a reader can refer to the picture for help if he or she has difficulty with an unknown word.

pragmatics

The understanding that context influences meaning. A reader with a strong grasp of pragmatics understands that a sentence can have different meanings depending on the situation or context in which it is used, including, for example, the tone of voice of a speaker. For example, a sentence can be a mere statement, an affirmation, a warning, a promise, or a threat.

primary division

Grades 1 to 3 in Ontario.

primary language

The first language a child learns to speak. This report uses the terms "first language" or "home language".

print awareness

Awareness of the rules of written language, such as knowing that letters and numbers convey meaning and that words are separated by spaces.

provincial standard

Level 3 of the four levels of achievement, as specified in the Ontario curriculum. Level 3 indicates a high level of achievement, or between B– and B+. (*Also see* **achievement levels**.)

reading strategies

Methods used in reading to determine the meaning of a text. Examples include substituting an appropriate familiar word for an unfamiliar one, and using root words to determine unfamiliar words. (*See* Ontario Ministry of Education, *The Ontario Curriculum, Grades 1–8: Language*, 1997.)

rime

The part of a syllable that contains the vowel and all that follows it. A rime is smaller than a syllable but larger than a phoneme. For example: b*one* and t*one*.

rubric

A scoring scale that provides a set of criteria for achievement and descriptions of levels of achievement, used to evaluate students' work or to guide students to desired performance levels. The rubric makes the scoring of student work more precise by providing clear descriptions of work at each of the levels of performance. (*See* **achievement levels**.)

running record

A method of observing, scoring, and analysing a child's reading aloud. A running record allows a teacher to record and then analyse reading behaviours.

self-assessment

Students' own assessment of their personal progress in knowledge, skills, or processes relative to the expectations in the curriculum.

semantics

The study of meaning in language, including the meaning of words, phrases, and sentences.

shared leadership

See **distributed leadership**.

shared reading

A method of instruction in which the teacher uses enlarged books or text that all students can see (such as overhead transparencies, commercial and class-made big books, pocket charts, posters, charts, and murals) so that the students can follow along as the teacher reads. The text is read several times, and students are encouraged to join in the reading.

sight word

A word that a child recognizes and reads instantly without having to sound it out.

standard

A description of student performance that outlines a particular level of achievement of the curriculum expectations. In Ontario, level 3 is the provincial standard.

syllable

The smallest part that a word can be divided into that includes a vowel. For example, "watermelon" has four syllables: wa-ter-mel-on.

syntax

The way words are combined to form phrases, clauses, or sentences. The syntax of a language includes both classes of words (such as nouns, verbs, and adjectives) and their functions (such as subject and object).

synthesis

The putting together of the constituent parts or elements to form a new whole.

volunteers

Members of a school's community who may or may not be professionally qualified as teachers but who nevertheless offer their time to help teachers in schools and classes.

whole school approach

A process by which all members of a school (including students and parents) work together, drawing on their different perspectives and responsibilities, to achieve common goals.

word identification

The ability to read familiar words automatically. (*See* **word knowledge**.)

word knowledge

The ability to use word identification strategies to read partially familiar or unfamiliar words. (*See* **word identification**.)

word study

A method of instruction that gives children the opportunity to practise high-frequency words so that they can read them automatically (word identification), and to learn word-solving strategies so that they will be able to read partially familiar or unfamiliar words (word knowledge).

word wall

An alphabetic list of words, displayed prominently in the classroom, that teachers use to help children recognize high-frequency words when reading and spell those words correctly when writing.

Sources and Suggested Readings

Adams, M. J. (1990). *Beginning to read: Thinking and learning about print.* Urbana-Champaign, IL: University of Illinois.

Adams, M. J., Foorman, B. R., Lundberg, I., & Becker, T. (1998). The elusive phoneme. *American Educator, 22*(1), 18–31.

Allington, R. L. (1983). Fluency: The neglected reading goal. *The Reading Teacher, 36*(6): 556–561.

Allington, R. L. (2002). What I've learned about effective reading instruction. *Phi Delta Kappan, 83*(10), 740–747.

Allington, R. L. & Cunningham, P. (1996). *Schools that work: Where all children read and write.* New York: Harper Collins.

Alves Martins, M., & Selva, C. (2001). Le rôle de la conscience phonologique dans l'apprentissage de la lecture : Apports et limites. In G. Chauveau (Ed.), *Comprendre l'enfant apprenti lecteur : recherches actuelles en psychologie de l'écrit* (pp. 89–100). Paris: Retz.

American Federation of Teachers. (1999). *Making standards matter 1999: An update on state activity* (AFT educational issues, Policy Brief No. 11). Washington, DC: Author.

American Federation of Teachers. (1999). *Teaching reading IS rocket science.* Washington, DC: Author.

Baker, L., & Brown, A. L. (2001). Metacognitive skills and reading. In P. D. Pearson, R. Barr, M. L. Kamil, and P. Mosenthal (Eds.), *Handbook of reading research* (Vol. 1, pp. 353–394). Mahwah, NJ: Lawrence Erlbaum Associates. (Original work published 1984).

Beck, I. L., McKeown, M. G., Hamilton, R. L., & Kucan, L. (1998). Getting at the meaning: How to help students unpack difficult text. *American Educator, 22*(1), 66–71 and 85.

Biemiller, A. (1999). *Language and reading success.* Cambridge, MA: Brookline Books.

Biemiller, A. (2001). Teaching vocabulary: Early, direct, and sequential. *American Educator, 25*(1), 24–28 and 47.

Blachowicz, C., & Ogle, D. (2001). *Reading comprehension: Strategies for independent learners.* New York: Guilford.

Bloom, B. S., & Kathwohl, D. R. (1956). *Taxonomy of educational objectives: The classification of educational goals: Handbook I, cognitive domain.* New York: Longman, Green.

Booth, A., & Dunn, J. R. (Eds.). (1996). *Family-school links: How do they affect educational outcomes?* Mahweh, NJ: Lawrence Erlbaum.

Brisk, M. E., and Harrington, M. M. (2000). *Literacy and bilingualism: A handbook for ALL teachers.* Mahwah, NJ: Lawrence Erlbaum Associates.

Burns, M. S., Griffin P., & Snow, C. E. (Eds.). (1999). *Starting out right: a guide to promoting children's reading success.* Washington, DC: National Academies Press.

California Department of Education. (1995). *Every child a reader* (Report of the California Reading Task Force). Sacramento: Author.

Calkins, L. M. (2001). *The art of teaching reading*. New York: Longman.

Center for the Improvement of Early Reading Achievement. (2001). *Put reading first: The research building blocks for teaching children to read: Kindergarten through grade 3*. Washington, DC: The Partnership for Reading (National Institute for Literacy, National Institute of Child Health and Human Development, Department of Education).

Centre franco-ontarien des ressources pédagogiques. (1998). *Trousse d'intervention précoce en lecture*. Ottawa: Author.

Centre franco-ontarien des ressources pédagogiques. (2002). *La gestion, l'amélioration, la profession – Jardin d'enfants – Écoles élémentaires publiques de langue française de l'Ontario*. Ottawa: Author.

Centre franco-ontarien des ressources pédagogiques. (2002). *La gestion, l'amélioration, la profession – Jardin d'enfants – Écoles élémentaires catholiques de langue française de l'Ontario*. Ottawa: Author.

Centre franco-ontarien des ressources pédagogiques. (2002). *La gestion, l'amélioration, la profession – 1ère année – Écoles élémentaires publiques de langue française de l'Ontario*. Ottawa: Author.

Centre franco-ontarien des ressources pédagogiques. (2002). *La gestion, l'amélioration, la profession – 1ère année – Écoles élémentaires catholiques de langue française de l'Ontario*. Ottawa: Author.

Centre franco-ontarien des ressources pédagogiques. (2002). *La gestion, l'amélioration, la profession – 2e année – Écoles élémentaires publiques de langue française de l'Ontario*. Ottawa: Author.

Centre franco-ontarien des ressources pédagogiques. (2002). *La gestion, l'amélioration, la profession – 2e année – Écoles élémentaires catholiques de langue française de l'Ontario*. Ottawa: Author.

Centre franco-ontarien des ressources pédagogiques. (2002). *La gestion, l'amélioration, la profession – 3e année – Écoles élémentaires publiques de langue française de l'Ontario*. Ottawa: Author.

Centre franco-ontarien des ressources pédagogiques. (2002). *La gestion, l'amélioration, la profession – 3e année – Écoles élémentaires catholiques de langue française de l'Ontario*. Ottawa: Author.

Chall, J. S. (1996). *Stages of reading development* (2nd ed.). Fort Worth, TX: Harcourt Brace.

Clay, M. M. (1991). *Becoming literate: The construction of inner control*. Portsmouth, NH: Heinemann.

Clay, M. M. (1993). *An observation survey of early literacy achievement*. Portsmouth, NH: Heinemann.

Clay, M. M. (2000). *Running records for classroom teachers*. Portsmouth, NH: Heinemann.

Clay, M. M. (2003). *Le sondage d'observation en lecture-écriture*. Montreal: Chenelière/McGraw-Hill.

Comer, J., & Haynes, M. (1991). Parent involvement in schools: An ecological approach. *Elementary School Journal, 91*(3), 271–277.

Commonwealth of Australia. (1997). *Literacy standards in Australia*. Canberra: Author.

Consortium régional de l'Est de l'Ontario. (1997). *Dépistage précoce et continu : Bilan des forces et des faiblesses d'un ou d'une élève*. Ottawa: Author.

Cunningham, A. E., & Stanovich, K. S. (1998). What reading does for the mind. *American Educator, 22*(1), 8–15.

Delpit, L. D. (1995). *Other people's children: Cultural conflict in the classroom*. New York: New Press.

Department for Education and Skills, England. (1998). *The National Literacy Strategy: Framework for teaching YR to Y6*. London: Author.

Develay, M. (1996). *Donner du sens à l'école*. Paris: ESF.

Education Quality and Accountability Office. (2002). *EQAO guide to school and board improvement planning*. Toronto: Author.

Elmore, R. F. (2000). *Building a new structure for school leadership*. Washington, DC: Albert Shankar Institute.

Elmore, R. F. (2002). *Bridging the gap between standards and achievement: The imperative for professional development in education*. Washington, DC: Albert Shankar Institute.

Falk, B. (2002). Standards-based reforms: Problems and possibilities. *Phi Delta Kappan, 83*(8), 612–620.

Fountas, I. C. (1999). Matching books to readers: *Using leveled books in guided reading, K–3*. Portsmouth, NH: Heinemann.

Fountas, I. C. (2001). *Guided readers and writers, grades 3–6*. Portsmouth, NH: Heinemann.

Fountas, I. C., & Pinnell, G. S. (1996). *Guided reading: Good first teaching for all children*. Portsmouth, NH: Heinemann.

Fullan, M. (1993). *Change forces: Probing the depth of educational reform*. New York: Falmer Press.

Gambrell, L. (1996). Creating classroom cultures that foster reading motivation. *The Reading Teacher, 50*(1), 14–25.

Giasson, J. (1990). *La compréhension en lecture*. Boucherville, QC: Gaëtan Morin.

Giasson, J. (1995). *La lecture : De la théorie à la pratique*. Boucherville, QC: Gaëtan Morin.

Guthrie, J. T. (1996). Educational contexts for engagement in literacy. *The Reading Teacher, 49*(6), 432–445.

Halliday, M. A. K. (1973). *Explorations in the functions of language*. London: Edward Arnold.

Harvey, S., & Goudvis, A. (2000). *Strategies that work: Teaching comprehension to enhance understanding*. Portland, ME: Stenhouse.

Heibert, E. H., & Raphael, T. (1997). *Early literacy instruction*. Fort Worth, TX: Harcourt Brace.

Hill, P. W., & Crévola, C. A. (1999). The role of standards in educational reform for the 21st century. In D. D. Marsh (Ed.), *ASCD Yearbook: Preparing our schools for the 21st century*. Retrieved December 10, 2002, from Association for Supervision and Curriculum Development website at http://www.ascd.org/readingroom/books/marsh99toc.html.

International Reading Association. (2000). *Excellent reading teacher* (Position statement). Washington, DC: Author.

International Reading Association. (2002). *Family-school partnerships: Essential elements of literacy instruction in the United States*. Newark, DE: Author.

International Reading Association and National Association for the Education of Young Children. (1998). *Learning to read and write: Developmentally appropriate practices for young children* (Position statement). Washington, DC: Author.

Lambert, L. (1998). *Building leadership capacity in schools*. Washington, DC: Association for Supervision and Curriculum Development.

Lawlor, D. (1991). *Parent-teacher conferencing in early childhood education*. Washington, DC: Association for Supervision and Curriculum Development.

Learning First Alliance. (1998). *Every child reading: An action plan*. Washington, DC: Author.

Learning First Alliance. (2000). *Every child reading: A professional development guide*. Washington, DC: Author.

Lipps, G., & Yiptong-Avila, J. (1999). *From home to school – How Canadian children cope: Initial analysis using data from the second cycle of the School Component of the National Longitudinal Survey of Children and Youth*. Ottawa: Statistics Canada.

Lyons, C. A., & Pinnell, G. S. (2001). *Systems for change in literacy education: A guide to professional development*. Portsmouth, NH: Heinemann.

Maria, K. (1989). Developing disadvantaged children's background knowledge interactively. *The Reading Teacher, 42*(4), 296–300.

McLaughlin, M., & Allen, M. B. (2002). *Guided comprehension: A teaching model for grades 3–8*. Newark, DE: International Reading Association.

Ministère de l'Éducation de l'Ontario. (1994). *Actualisation linguistique en français et perfectionnement du français*. Toronto: Author.

Ministère de l'Éducation de l'Ontario. (1994). *Aménagement linguistique en français*. Toronto: Author.

Ministère de l'Éducation de l'Ontario. (1994). *Investir dans l'animation culturelle*. Toronto: Author.

Ministère de l'Éducation de l'Ontario. (1997). *Français : Le curriculum de l'Ontario de la 1re à la 8e année*. Toronto: Author.

Moats, L. C. (1998). Teaching decoding. *American Educator, 22*(1), 42–49 and 95–96.

National Reading Panel. (2000). *Teaching children to read: An evidence-based assessment of the scientific research literature on reading and its implications for reading instruction*. Washington, DC: National Institute of Child Health and Human Development, and Department of Education.

Ontario Ministry of Education. (1997). *The Ontario curriculum, grades 1–8: Language*. Toronto: Author.

Ontario Ministry of Education. (1998). *Guide to the Provincial Report Card, Grades 1–8*. Toronto: Author.

Ontario Ministry of Education. (1998). *The kindergarten program*. Toronto: Author.

Ontario Ministry of Education. (2000). *The Ontario curriculum – Exemplars, grades 1–8: Reading*. Toronto: Author.

Ontario Ministry of Education. (2001). *Early reading: A guide to setting targets for student achievement*. Toronto: Author.

Ontario Ministry of Education. (2001). *Helping your child learn to read: A parent's guide*. Toronto: Early Reading Strategy, Author.

O'Sullivan, J., & Howe, M. L. (1999). *Overcoming poverty: Promoting literacy in children from low-income families* (A Research Report for the National Literacy Secretariat, Human Resources Development Canada). Thunder Bay, ON: Lakehead University.

Ouzoulias, A. (2001). L'émergence de la conscience phonémique: apprentissage sensoriel ou développement conceptuel? In G. Chauveau (Ed.), *Comprendre l'enfant apprenti lecteur : recherches actuelles en psychologie de l'écrit* (pp. 101–127). Paris: Retz.

Palinscar, A. S., & Brown, A. L. (1984). Reciprocal teaching of comprehension fostering and monitoring activities. *Cognition and Instruction, 1*, 117–175.

Paris, S., & Winograd, P. (1990). How metacognition can promote academic learning and instruction. In B. F. Jones & L. Idol (Eds.), *Dimensions of thinking and cognitive instruction* (pp.1–44). Mahwah, NJ: Lawrence Erlbaum Associates.

Partnership for Family Involvement in Education. (1999). *A compact for reading guide: A reading partnership action kit*. Washington, DC: US Department of Education and the Los Angeles Times.

Partnership for Reading. (2001). *Put reading first: Helping your child learn to read: A parent guide: Preschool through grade 3*. Washington, DC: Author (National Institute for Literacy, National Institute of Child Health and Human Development, Department of Education).

Peregoy, S., & Boyle, O. (2001). *Reading, writing and learning in ESL: A resource book for K–12 teachers*. New York: Longman.

Perrenoud, P. (1997). *Construire des compétences dès l'école*. Issy-les-Moulineaux, France: ESF.

Perrenoud, P. (2000). *Pédagogique différenciée : Des intentions à l'action*. Issy-les-Moulineaux, France: ESF.

Pressley, M. (2002). *Reading instruction that works: The case for balanced teaching* (2nd ed.). New York: Guilford.

Raphael, T. E. (1984). Teaching learners about sources of information for answering comprehension questions. *Journal of Reading, 27*(4), 303–311.

Rupley, W. H., Logan, J. W., & Nichols, W. D. (1998–99). Vocabulary instruction in a balanced reading program. *The Reading Teacher, 52*(4), 336–346.

Saskatchewan Education. (1997). *Building communities of hope: Best practices for meeting the learning needs of at-risk and Indian and Métis students: Communities schools policy and conceptual framework*. Regina SK: Author.

Saskatchewan Education. (1997). *Building communities of hope: Implementation handbook*. Regina SK: Author.

Scottish Office. (1998). *Raising standards – setting targets: Primary schools support pack: Taking a closer look at 5–14 attainment in primary schools*. Edinburgh: Author.

Snow, C. E. (2002). *Reading for understanding: Toward an R&D program in reading comprehension*. Arlington, VA: RAND.

Snow, C. E., Burns, M. S., & Griffin, P. (Eds.). (1999). *Preventing reading difficulties in young children*. Washington, DC: National Research Council, Committee on the Prevention of Reading Difficulties in Young Children.

Snow, C. E., & Tabors, P. O. (1993). Language skills that relate to literacy development. In B. Spodek & O. N. Saracho (Eds.), *Language and literacy in early childhood education* (pp.1–20). New York: Teachers College Press.

Stanovich, K. E. (1986). Matthew effects in reading: Some consequences of individual differences in the acquisition of literacy. *Reading Research Quarterly, 21*(4), 360–406.

Stanovich, K. E. (1994). Romance and reality. *The Reading Teacher, 47*(4), 280–291.

Swick, K. J. (1991). *Teacher-parent partnerships to enhance school success in early childhood education*. Washington, DC: National Education Association, and Southern Early Childhood Association.

Swick, K. J. (1992). *An early childhood school-home learning design*. Champaign, IL: Stipes Publishing.

Swick, K. J., & Graves, S. B. (1993). *Empowering at-risk families during the early childhood years*. Washington, DC: National Education Association.

Tardif, J. (1996). *Pour un enseignement stratégique : L'apport de la psychologie cognitive*. Montreal: Les Éditions logiques.

Tardif, J. (1999). *Le transfert des apprentissages*. Montreal: Les Éditions logiques.

Texas Education Agency, Texas Reading Initiative. (n. d.). *Beginning reading instruction: Practical ideas for parents*. Austin, TX: Author.

Turner, J., & Paris, S. G. (1995). How literacy tasks influence children's motivation for literacy. *The Reading Teacher, 48*(8), 662–673.

US Department of Education. (1996). *Achieving the goals: Goal 4: Teacher professional development*. Retrieved December 10, 2002, from US Department of Education website at http://www.ed.gov/pubs/AchGoal4/intro.html.

Van Grunderbeeck, V. (1994). *Les difficultés en lecture : Diagnostic et pistes d'intervention*. Boucherville, QC: Gaëtan Morin.

Willis, A. I. (2000). *Critical issue: Addressing literacy needs in culturally and linguistically diverse classrooms*. Retrieved December 10, 2002, from North Central Regional Educational Laboratory website at http://www.ncrel.org/sdrs/areas/issues/content/cntareas/reading/li400.htm.

Willows, D. (2002). The balanced literary diet. *The School Administrator 59*(1), 30–33.